HORRIBLE SCIENCE

THE FEARSOME FIGHT

FLIGHT

NICK ARNOLD

Illustrated by
Tony De Saulles

C0000002915614

Scholastic Children's Books,
Euston House, 24 Eversholt Street,
London NW1 1DB, UK
A division of Scholastic UK Ltd
London ~ New York ~ Toronto ~ Sydney ~ Auckland
Mexico City ~ New Delhi ~ Hong Kong

First published in the UK by Scholastic UK Ltd, 2004

Text copyright © Nick Arnold, 2004
Illustrations copyright © Tony De Saulles, 2004

10 digit ISBN 0 439 97362 7
13 digit ISBN 978 0439 97362 5

Printed and bound by Nørhaven Paperback A/S, Denmark

4 6 8 10 9 7 5 3

The rights of Nick Arnold and Tony De Saulles to be identified as the author and
illustrator of this work respectively have been asserted by them in accordance
with the Copyright, Designs and Patents Act, 1988.

Contents

WHAAAAAAAAA!

Nick Arnold has been writing stories and books since he was a youngster, but never dreamt he'd find fame writing about flight. His research involved making a parachute jump and he enjoyed every minute of it.

When he's not delving into Horrible Science, he spends his spare time eating pizza, riding his bike and thinking up corny jokes (though not all at the same time).

Tony De Saulles picked up his crayons when he was still in nappies and has been doodling ever since. He takes Horrible Science very seriously and even agreed to test a Flying Flea plane. Fortunately, he has made a full recovery.

When he's not out with his sketchpad, Tony likes to write poetry and play squash, though he hasn't written any poetry about squash yet.

INTRODUCTION

This foolish man is about to test a dodgy home-made pair of wings…

SMASHING NEW INVENTION…

HOP!

SMASH!

Well, what do you expect? Humans aren't designed to fly – as you can find out in this book. It's called *The Fearsome Fight for Flight* because it tells the story of the battle to build flying machines. We'll be reliving the terror, the triumphs and the tears, and finding out why hundreds of people got killed. Our route will cover…

• The death-defying facts about flying.
• The blood-curdling blunders of barmy balloons and awesome airships.
• The fearsome flops of human-powered flight.

• The dreadful downfalls of grisly gliders (aeroplanes without engines).
• The plane-crazy perils of aeroplanes, jets and hair-raising helicopters.
• And the fateful future of flight.

This book's sure to be scary and exciting, and by the time you've finished it, you'll have logged more fearsome facts than the average teacher tots up in a lifetime. But afterwards you may find yourself thinking more about flight – and even whether air travel is a good thing…

We'll be taking off very soon, but first here are a few vital safety announcements…

THIS BOOK INCLUDES GRISLY GRUESOME BITS. YOU MAY WANT TO KEEP YOUR SICK BAG HANDY!

Another safety warning…

This book is designed for reading only and should not be used as…

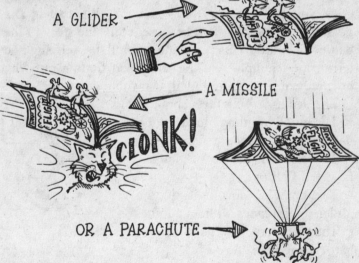

A GLIDER

A MISSILE

CLONK!

OR A PARACHUTE

There is some science in this book, but it's been cushioned with lots of jokes to stop it damaging your brain too much.

Yet another safety warning…
We'd like to warn readers that it's a very BAD idea to try to copy the crazy people and stupid stunts in this book. Yes, only airheads prance around on the wings of an aircraft 1,000 metres in the air. And as for leaping off tall buildings armed with a pair of feathery wings … that's only suitable for bird-brains.

Provided you follow these warnings, this book is perfectly safe to read. You may feel an urge to giggle – but this is perfectly normal. In fact, the jokes have been tested on teachers and, although rather old, they're very reliable (and that goes for the jokes too!).

Well, thank you for listening… You are now cleared to fly. So, if you'll kindly fasten your safety belt and turn the page, we can take to the air…

Have a HORRIBLE flight!

DEATH-DEFYING FLYING FACTS

This chapter is all about why planes fly and don't flop out of the sky like soggy pancakes. But before we get to grips with their soaraway secrets, let's check out how it feels to fly...

The date: TODAY
The time: EVENING
The place: ANY AIRPORT IN THE WORLD

You're about to fly. Your plane waits on the runway like a high jumper ready for their run-up.

How do you feel? Tense? Nervous? Just a teeny-weeny bit scared? Will the plane *really* fly? you worry. Or will it plummet from the sky with a crash, a bang and a splat? And how can anything as heavy as a plane fly anyway?

All is silent except for the whining engines. Then they moan louder and louder until they set your teeth on edge. The plane starts to move. The engines throb and roar, and all at once the plane races forward. You see the airfield hurtle past – it's all a blur and, before you know it, the plane soars upwards.

Your ears pop as the ground drops away and the plane climbs towards the rolling clouds. Then, all at once, you're as high as the clouds and the ground is a map seen from above. Up in the dark evening sky, a lone star gleams…

Yes – flying is magic! I mean when you fly you get to see loads of things that you don't normally see. Stuff like…

• The tops of the clouds.

• The sun shining *above* the clouds.

And if you're really lucky you could get to see…
• The sunset for the SECOND time in a day. (If you take off after sunset, the sun reappears as you fly higher.)

• The shadow of the Earth. (You can see the curving shadow to the east on the tops of clouds after sunset.)

But the most amazing sensation is to have nothing under your feet. Nothing except for the plane floor and 7,000 metres of empty air.

9

A quick note about heights…

I hope you're not scared of heights, because there are lots of hair-raising heights and dizzying drops in this book. Here are a few to get you worried…

11,300 METRES — HIGHEST FLYING BIRD (A VULTURE), WAS HIT BY A PLANE IN 1973.

SPLAT!

10,000 METRES — WISPY CIRRUS CLOUDS.

POOR BERT!

8,800 METRES — MOUNT EVEREST.

1,800 METRES — TOP OF "COTTON-WOOL" CUMULUS (CUE-MU-LUS) CLOUD.
1,400 METRES — BASE OF CUMULUS CLOUD.

320 METRES — EIFFEL TOWER.

C'EST TRÈS HAUTE!

0.4 METRES — HEIGHT OF YOUR CHAIR (UNLESS YOU HAPPEN TO BE SITTING IN A HIGH CHAIR).

5 METRES — A GIRAFFE.

YES, I AM!

HI!

It feels scary but thrilling to fly so high. And to get this thrill, people have lost their lives and broken their legs and done terrible things to puppies and kittens. But before we get to grips with these fearsome facts, we need to find out exactly how planes fly…

A crash course in how planes fly
We've asked brainy boffins Professor N Large and Wanda Wye to build us a plane…

And now all we need is a fearless pilot to show us how it flies… Any volunteers? Well, we've just heard of a hard-up, hard-boiled, New York private eye who'll do anything for cash…

As luck would have it, MI Gutzache used to be a pilot but he quit for some reason. Anyway, he's agreed to find out how planes fly…

Er, sorry about Mr Gutzache's sickening problem. Here are the forces involved in flying…

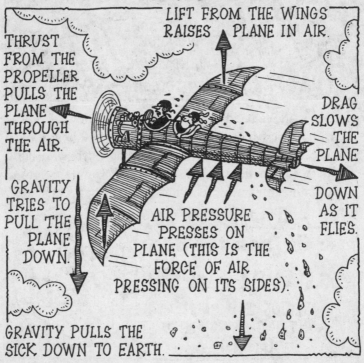

Fearsome expressions

A scientist says…

Do you say…?

I STUDY THE SCIENCE OF DRAG

MY SCIENCE LESSONS ARE A DRAG TOO!

Answer:
Say that and the scientist might drag you around his lab! Drag is the force made by air hitting something flying through the air. It affects planes and birds and underpants blowing off your teacher's washing line. And the faster the object flies, the harder drag tries to slow it down.

But what is this mysterious "lift" that raises the plane in the air? Well, in order to make sense of lift we need to know that air is made of countless tiny clumps of atoms called molecules (moll-eck-ules). They spend their time zooming about.

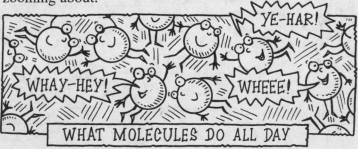

YE-HAR!

WHAY-HEY!

WHEEE!

WHAT MOLECULES DO ALL DAY

13

And now we can take a look at lift in action. Let's see what those air molecules are up to around the wings of Gutzache's plane…

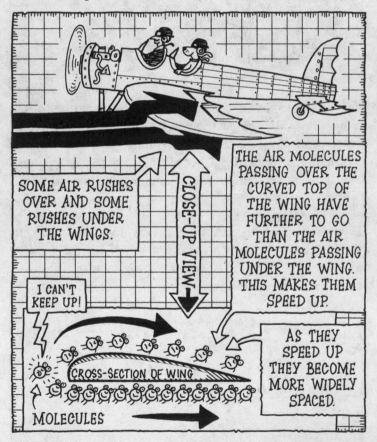

SOME AIR RUSHES OVER AND SOME RUSHES UNDER THE WINGS.

CLOSE-UP VIEW

THE AIR MOLECULES PASSING OVER THE CURVED TOP OF THE WING HAVE FURTHER TO GO THAN THE AIR MOLECULES PASSING UNDER THE WING. THIS MAKES THEM SPEED UP.

I CAN'T KEEP UP!

CROSS-SECTION OF WING

AS THEY SPEED UP THEY BECOME MORE WIDELY SPACED.

MOLECULES

The force of air pressure becomes weaker above the wing than under it. And BINGO – the air pressure under the wing lifts the wing (and the plane) higher! Yes, every plane in the world stays up with the help of tiny air molecules!

Phew – did you get all that? Oh well, it's easy to remember. You get a lift in a plane and the plane gets a lift from its wings. And now for a quick quiz to "lift" your spirits...

The wing shape, curved on top and flatter underneath, is called an aerofoil. Which TWO of the following has an aerofoil shape?

a) A ski-jumper's body

b) A flying custard pie
c) A boomerang

Answer:
a) YES. Ski jumpers lean forward as they fly to make an aerofoil shape. This keeps them in the air for longer.
b) NO … and don't go chucking one at your little sister to find out.
c) YES, the aerofoil shape of the boomerang makes it glide through the air at 160 km per hour.

Bet you never knew!
Native Australians used boomerangs for hunting animals. The thin edge of the boomerang came in handy for cutting open the skins of dead animals in order to get at the tasty heart, kidneys and liver.

But of course a plane can only get lift to fly if it has wings. So can you guess what would happen if the wings fell off while the plane was flying? Well, it's just happened to MI Gutzache and Watson…

16

Without wings, the plane loses lift and Gutzache and Watson have to leap for their lives. Only drag slows them down as they fall – but luckily they're wearing parachutes. The parachutes open and trap billions of air molecules, massively increasing the force of drag and slowing their fall. So they have a nice soft landing…

Well, that was scientifically interesting – by the way, I wonder where Gutzache's sick landed?

Now I bet you can't wait to build a plane that'll fly better than the Professor and Wanda Wye's effort – and you can on page 109. But first you'll need a bit more technical know-how, so let's start with two simple experiments…

Dare you discover … how life can be a drag?
What you need:
Two pieces of paper (but *don't* use your science homework and DEFINITELY don't tear pages from this book). The pieces of paper should be the same size.

What you do:
1 Screw up one of the pieces of paper. (I warned you *not* to use your science homework!)
2 Hold one piece of paper in each hand. Hold them as high as you can…
3 And drop them a few times…

You should notice:
The screwed-up paper ALWAYS hits the ground first. The flat sheet may see-saw or glide through the air. It falls more slowly because it has a larger surface area for billions of air molecules to push against.

Dare you discover ... how to make a flying saucer?

What you need:

A polystyrene party or picnic plate (better make sure there isn't a custard pie on it before you throw it!)

Eight 1p coins (It might be worth asking for £1 coins. They're not useful for the experiment, but they are useful for spending!)

Sticky tape

Scissors (plus a helpful adult to help with cutting)

What you do:

1 Use the sticky tape to stick the coins to the rim of the plate as shown.

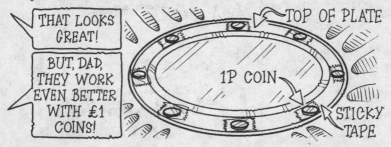

2 Practise throwing the plate upside down. (That's holding the plate upside down, NOT standing on your head!) By the way, you only need a gentle waft of your wrist to throw the plate. It doesn't work if you chuck it.

3 Throw the plate the right way up.

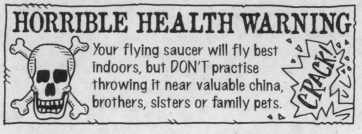

HORRIBLE HEALTH WARNING

Your flying saucer will fly best indoors, but DON'T practise throwing it near valuable china, brothers, sisters or family pets.

CRACK!

You should notice:

1 When you throw it upside down, the plate should glide smoothly through the air. If it doesn't, flick it more gently. Upside down, it forms an aerofoil shape and flies like the well-known toy called a frisbee.

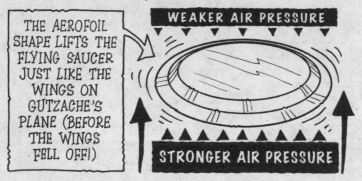

THE AEROFOIL SHAPE LIFTS THE FLYING SAUCER JUST LIKE THE WINGS ON GUTZACHE'S PLANE (BEFORE THE WINGS FELL OFF!)

WEAKER AIR PRESSURE

STRONGER AIR PRESSURE

2 When it's the right way up, the plate doesn't have an aerofoil shape and so it crashes.

THIS IS GETTING RIDICULOUS!

FLOP!

But frisbees aren't the only things that glide – birds such as seagulls glide, too (as you'll find out on page 71). Birds glide and fly so well because their wings are aerofoil shaped. And now here's a pigeon to explain how they compare to planes…

Bet you never knew!

1 According to legend, in 1500 BC King Kai Kaoos of Persia was flown to China by eagles tied to his throne. The eagles were flapping after some goat's meat stuck on spears just out of reach. Sadly, when they got to China the birds guzzled the meat and the miserable monarch was stuck in the desert.

2 But that didn't stop an inventor in Baltimore, USA. In 1865 he dreamt up an eagle-powered flying machine. The eagles could be steered using cords but they might not have worked if the eagles had spotted a tasty rabbit far below...

Psst – I'll let you into a secret! These machines were as useless as a hamster in a body-building contest. In fact, all attempts to fly like a bird with flapping wings risked a messy death. Which is a bit scary, because a little bird tells me the next chapter is full of them. Oh well, at least it's got parachutes in it too!

BIG-BRAINED BIRD MEN AND PLUNGING PARACHUTES

Have you ever had a secret urge to be a bird?

Me neither – I mean, I don't even like budgie seed! But that's probably how the story of human flight began – people looking at birds and longing to soar into the sky as free as a … er, bird. And they told stories about people who could fly. Let's look at these dusty old legends…

Hmm, maybe they're a bit *too* dusty.

ESCAPE FROM CRETE

Daedalus was the greatest inventor in Greece, but he had a problem. He was stuck on the island of Crete and its mean-minded king, Minos, wasn't going to let him and his son Icarus leave.

"What more do you want, Your Majesty?" grumbled Daedalus. "I've designed a maze for your half-human, half-bull monster to live in. Now I want to go home!"

"Ha ha, you'll have to fly first," jeered the cruel king.

That gave Daedalus an idea, and secretly he built two pairs of wings from feathers and wax — one for Icarus and one for himself.

"Now, son," said Daedalus. "These wings are our ticket out of here. They've only got one problem — the wax melts easily, so don't you go flying too close to the sun."

"I won't!" promised Icarus.

One morning, before King Minos's men could stop them, the brave pair launched themselves from a cliff and flew over the sea.

"Whee! This is COOL!" laughed Icarus as he whizzed over the waves like a seagull. On and on they flew, but Icarus forgot his promise and began to soar higher and higher until he was close to the sun. The heat melted the wax, which dripped from the wings. And before Daedalus could save him, the wings fell to bits.

With a cry of horror, Icarus plunged from the sky like a sack of potatoes.

AARRGGGGGGGH — SPLOSH! He hit the sea far below. And that was the end of him. Daedalus made it to Greece, but he spent the rest of his days mourning his lost son. And he never flew anywhere again...

THE HAPPY HAT TRICK

Young Shun had a problem. His dad didn't like him BIG TIME and had him locked up. Shun escaped disguised as a bird, but his dreaded dad caught him. The boy escaped a second time, this time disguised as a dragon... Now, if you ask me, the guards must have been a bit dozy. I mean, wouldn't you notice if a giant goose hopped past your nose? And wouldn't you look twice if a huge scaly dragon slithered over your shoes? Anyway, Shun's dad wasn't too impressed by his son's acting ability and decided to do him in.

So he locked poor Shun in a high tower and set it on fire. Surely, thought the dastardly dad, this time I'll cook Shun's goose (and his dragon too). But Shun had one more card to play...

Seizing two big reed hats, the boy leapt fearlessly from the tower and floated harmlessly to the ground. And after that you won't be too surprised to know that Shun became Emperor of China and his dad... well, the legend doesn't say, but I hope he suffered a fearsome fate.

The reed hats were probably too small to act like parachutes and slow the boy's fall. But supposing they were extra-large hats – it's just possible that the parachute was invented in ancient China!

As for the Daedalus story, that couldn't possibly be true. But don't take my word for it – here's our pigeon pal to tell us why humans can't fly like birds…

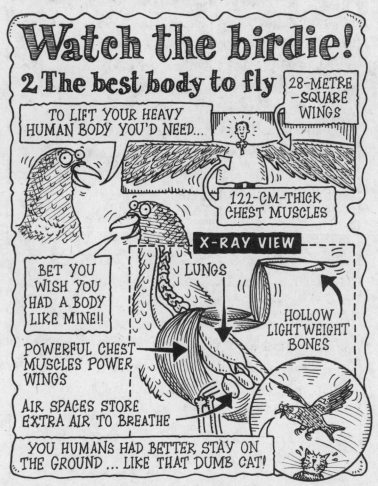

Watch the birdie!

2 The best body to fly

TO LIFT YOUR HEAVY HUMAN BODY YOU'D NEED...

28-METRE-SQUARE WINGS

122-CM-THICK CHEST MUSCLES

X-RAY VIEW

LUNGS

BET YOU WISH YOU HAD A BODY LIKE MINE!!

HOLLOW LIGHTWEIGHT BONES

POWERFUL CHEST MUSCLES POWER WINGS

AIR SPACES STORE EXTRA AIR TO BREATHE

YOU HUMANS HAD BETTER STAY ON THE GROUND ... LIKE THAT DUMB CAT!

Of course, if there'd been Horrible Science books 1,000 years ago, the people you're just about to meet might have read that last bit and decided to throw away their wings. But come to think of it, they were foolish enough to jump anyway...

Four foolish fall guys

1 Bladud
Date: 863 BC
Day job: King of Britain (according to legend). Educated in Athens and founder of the first English college. (If he invented schools, he sure had it coming.)

Flying machine: Feathered wings
Deadly downfall: Off the top of a temple.
Rotten result: SPLAT! Bloody for Blad.

2 Oliver of Malmesbury
Date: 1029
Day job: English monk
Flying machine: Feathered wings
Deadly downfall: Off the tower of Malmesbury Abbey.
Rotten result: Two broken legs. Oddball Ollie blamed his dangerous dive on not sticking a feathered tail on his battered bum.

3 Giovanni Battista Danti
Date: 1503
Day job:
Italian mathematician
Flying machine: Feathered wings
Deadly downfall: His first glide over a lake left him unhurt, so he celebrated by jumping off Perugia Cathedral.
Rotten result: Serious injury.

4 Marquis de Bacqueville
Date: 1742
Day job: French nobleman
Flying machine: Wings on his arms and legs
Deadly downfall: Tried to fly across the River Seine in Paris.
Rotten result: Crashed into a washerwoman's dirty old barge and broke both his legs.

The stick-insect-brained nobleman was described as…

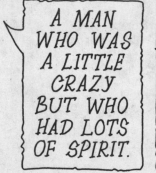

And you might say that about the rest of them too – and the dozens of other tower jumpers I haven't got time to tell you about. "So what's the answer?" I hear you cry. Well, they could have tied themselves to a giant kite…

Fearsome flight fact file

NAME: How a kite works

THE BASIC FACTS: 1 As a kite leans into the wind, the air molecules hit the underside of the kite and slide down it.

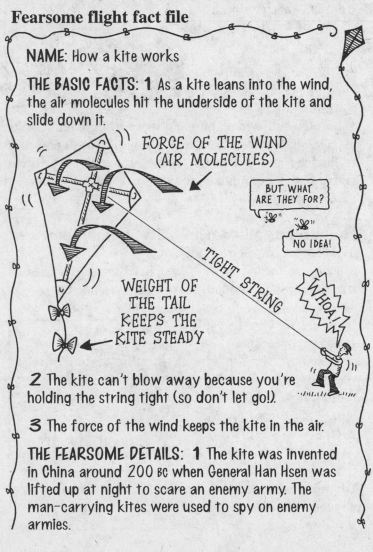

FORCE OF THE WIND
(AIR MOLECULES)

BUT WHAT ARE THEY FOR?

NO IDEA!

TIGHT STRING

WEIGHT OF THE TAIL KEEPS THE KITE STEADY

WHOA!

2 The kite can't blow away because you're holding the string tight (so don't let go!).

3 The force of the wind keeps the kite in the air.

THE FEARSOME DETAILS: 1 The kite was invented in China around 200 BC when General Han Hsen was lifted up at night to scare an enemy army. The man-carrying kites were used to spy on enemy armies.

2 According to Italian traveller Marco Polo (1254–1324), stupid or drunken men were picked for this perilous job. And some men were tied to kites as a punishment. Let's hope your ancient teacher doesn't think of this torture!

WHAAAAA!

I THINK SHE'S SORRY, SIR!

But for the half-witted, human-powered flight fans in this chapter, a kite was out of the question. It wasn't powered by humans and it was far too sensible. Some of them were dreaming of quite complicated machines – and they were even more silly…

The grand all-comers silly human-powered flying-machine competition

Grand prize for the silliest flying machine – free medical care (one way or another, you're going to need it!).

1 Vincent De Groof's combined parachute and flapping flying machine
Nationality: Belgian
Date: 1874

ARRRGH!

VINCENT DE GROOF GETTING IN A FLAP

Advantages: It worked the first time in Belgium as a parachute. Pity the flapping wings were useless.

Disadvantages: It didn't work in a later test over London. The frame broke and the machine was a dead loss. Sadly, De Groof was an even deader loss.

Judge's verdict: The machine isn't strong enough to fly. I'd rather bounce up and down on an exploding whoopee cushion than go up in that thing.

2 Leonardo da Vinci's flapping machine
Nationality: Italian
Date: About 1500

YES! YES! YES! YES! YES! ... NNNNO!

THE GROUND

Advantages: It looked kind of arty in Leo's sketch book – but then he was a great artist.

Disadvantages: If anyone had built it and flown it, they would have found they didn't have enough muscle power to flap the wings.

Judge's verdict: It would make a good exercise machine.

3 Jacob Degen's flapping flying machine and balloon
Nationality: Swiss
Date: 1809

IGNORE THIS BIT!

HE THINKS THAT ADDING WINGS WILL HELP HIM WING – I MEAN, WIN

Advantages: The machine hangs from a balloon, so it flies even if the wings don't work.

Disadvantages: The wings DON'T work.

Judge's verdict: Grr! This machine is a disgrace – using a balloon to fly is cheating! Degen is DISQUALIFIED and he's been suspended – er, hold on, he's already suspended from the balloon.

Bet you never knew!
In 1809 a crowd in Paris was so cross that Degen's invention wasn't a proper flying machine that they chased dodgy Degen out of town.

4 Dr WO Ayre's pedal-powered propeller thingie
Nationality: USA
Date: 1885

Advantages: It would make a great kiddie's climbing frame or even a bedstead. You had to pedal very hard to pump the tubes full of air that in turn powered the propellers – so it kept you fit.

Disadvantages: Everyone laughed at you.

Judge's verdict: The propellers would never get enough power to lift anything heavier than a hamster. But it's a worthy RUNNER-UP in our competition. It's almost silly enough to win … but not quite!

5 Jean Pierre Blanchard's sail-and pedal-powered flapping machine
Nationality: French
Date: 1781

PREPARE FOR TAKEOFF!

Advantages: Included a musician to play soothing music so you wouldn't get scared. Guaranteed 100 per cent safe. (It's too heavy to leave the ground!)
Disadvantages: See advantages. Especially the bit about not flying.
Judge's verdict: THE WINNER! Easily the most freaky flying machine ever – and it's even got in-flight entertainment!

GOLDEN BRICK AWARD

ZANK YOU!

Human-powered flight sounds a fatal flop, doesn't it? And so it was ... until the 1970s when scientists built a human-powered flying machine that flew. But a lot of things happened in the story of flight before then, so you'll have to hang on until page 139 to find out what happened. And no peeping!

In the meantime, the tower jumpers continued their deadly dives and the machine makers continued to create crazy contraptions. And the only reason more weren't killed was because their wings sometimes worked like Shun's hats – as parachutes. Pity they didn't work for poor de Groof.

Obviously the parachute is a vital bit of kit for every fearless flier – but who invented it? Well, experts argue about it until they're blue in the face and the question is a bit of a hot potato…

The fearsome fight to parachute

1485 Leonardo da Vinci designs a parachute but doesn't test it – any volunteers?

1779 Joseph Montgolfier makes a parachute and tests it by dropping a sheep from a tower. The sheep lands safely – now that's what I call a woolly jumper.

1785 Our pal Jean Pierre Blanchard experiments by tying a puppy to a parachute and dropping it from a balloon. (Don't try this at home.) The pup was fine, but as you'll find out on page 51, Blanchard was DOG-ged by misfortune.

1808 The parachute saves its first life when Polish balloonist Jordaki Kuparento makes a hasty exit when his balloon catches fire.

But early parachutes weren't all they were cracked up to be – and sometimes they did crack up. And my deeply dodgy mate, Honest Bob, wants to sell you some. Er, you'd best be warned – you may want to take what he tells you with a pinch of salt … or even a few tonnes of salt.

HONEST BOB'S PLANE PRODUCTS PRESENTS...

"You can trust Bob to look after your money – and he'll even spend it for you!" Bob's mum

LOVELY CHOICE OF PARACHUTES
(and they come in pretty colours, too)

1 André Garnerin's perfect parachute (1797)
This chute's a beaut! You stand in the basket and get a good view of the ground (before you hit it).

YOURS IS STEADIER!

2 Robert Cocking's parachute (1837)
It's a real classy mover! Guaranteed not to swing from side to side, and you can even use it as an umbrella.

YIKES... AND FASTER!

A couple of facts that Honest Bob left out...

1 Garnerin's parachute swayed a lot in the wind. Each time he tried it he swayed until he was sick – but at least he lived, unlike...

2 Robert Cocking. "I never felt more comfortable," declared the 61-year-old artist just before falling to his death when the parachute broke.

What's that? You feel your teacher or puppy or brother or sister would enjoy a parachute jump? You haven't asked them, but you feel sure they'd like the idea once they were plunging through the air...? Well, I think it's a good idea to find out how they might get on...

Dare you discover ... how to make your teacher try a parachute jump?

What you need:

Ruler

Biro and paper

Scissors (and the same helpful adult who helped with the cutting in the previous experiment – hopefully they weren't injured too badly)

Paper napkin (about 32 x 32 cm)

Blu-tack

Thread

Sticky tape

Paperclip

What you do:

1 Cut a piece of paper 4.5 cm long and 2 cm wide. Fold it as shown and draw your teacher on both sides.

2 Cut an 80-cm length of thread. Fold it in half lengthways and cut again to make two 40-cm lengths.

3 Thread one length of thread through the paperclip. Stick the ends of the threads to the napkin as shown.

36

4 Repeat step three with the second length of thread.

5 Make sure the paperclip is halfway along the lengths of thread and use a tiny blob of Blu-tack to stick the threads to the paperclip.

6 Place the napkin on the table so that the paperclip is underneath. Cut 7-cm corners off the napkin as shown.

7 Add the sticky tape as shown. Tuck the ends of the tape under the edges of the napkin.

8 Gently use the point of a biro to make a hole 0.5 cm across at the centre of the sticky-tape cross.

9 Slide the paper with your teacher's picture into the paperclip.

10 Now for the fun bit. Drop your teacher from a height! No, I didn't mean your real teacher!

You should find:

The parachute swings from side to side just like Garnerin's bucket chute. This happens because air trapped under the parachute tries to escape, pushing it from side to side. The hole lets air escape and stops the parachute from swaying too much – and that's why modern parachutes have holes in their tops...

OK, so you've found out how a parachute works – but how does it *feel* to make a jump? A US Air Corps scientist named Harry Armstrong made a jump and asked himself this very queasy question. Here's my version of his notes…

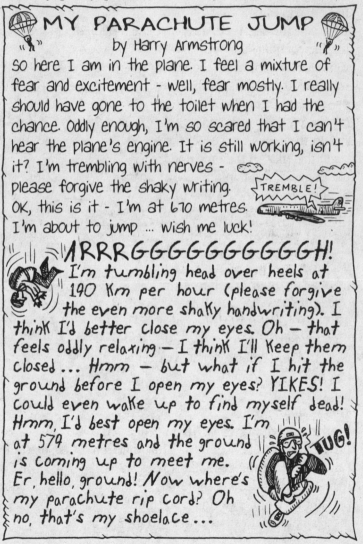

MY PARACHUTE JUMP
by Harry Armstrong

So here I am in the plane. I feel a mixture of fear and excitement - well, fear mostly. I really should have gone to the toilet when I had the chance. Oddly enough, I'm so scared that I can't hear the plane's engine. It is still working, isn't it? I'm trembling with nerves - please forgive the shaky writing. OK, this is it - I'm at 670 metres. I'm about to jump … wish me luck!

TREMBLE!

ARRRGGGGGGGGGGH! I'm tumbling head over heels at 190 Km per hour (please forgive the even more shaky handwriting). I think I'd better close my eyes. Oh – that feels oddly relaxing – I think I'll Keep them closed … Hmm – but what if I hit the ground before I open my eyes? YIKES! I could even wake up to find myself dead! Hmm, I'd best open my eyes. I'm at 579 metres and the ground is coming up to meet me. Er, hello, ground! Now where's my parachute rip cord? Oh no, that's my shoelace…

TUG!

And you'll be cheering out loud to hear that Harry landed safely. But the girl in our next story didn't look set for a happy landing. I've got three excuses to tell this terrible true tale…

a) It's exciting.

b) It was the first time anyone used a parachute to rescue another person.

c) It features a flying machine that you can find out about in the next crazy chapter.

The Daily News
— 1908 —

DARING DOLLY SAVES MAY'S DAY!

Daring parachute stunt jumper Dolly Shepherd and her friend Louie May faced certain death yesterday. As the girls dangled from an unmanned balloon 7,000 metres in the air, luckless Louie couldn't free her chute.

Daring Dolly (whose previous jobs include being a waitress and a target for a blindfolded sharp-shooter) bravely battled to free her friend.

When Louie was freed, the two girls jumped using Dolly's parachute. But they fell too fast and Dolly hurt her back. Said Dolly from her bed, "It gave me a nasty jolt – especially the landing. Ouch! My poor back! Where's me vapour rub?"

Dolly Shepherd

But you'll be jumping with joy to read that, four years later, Dolly realized that too many scary stunts would kill her, so she gave up parachuting. And she lived to the ripe old age of 97.

So, did you spot the flying machine we'll be talking about next? No? Huh! Well, here are a few more clues: it's big and round and filled with hot air or gas (which sometimes leaks). It can be dangerous…

NO! It's a balloon – so read on. The next chapter will take you to new heights…

BARMY BALL**OO**NS

OOER!

Balloons are a pretty sight as they sail silently through the skies – but the fight to fly them was far from pretty. We're about to take to the air with a curious crew of brilliantly barmy balloonists and be swept away on a gale of fearsome facts... Er, do you think this chapter's actually *safe*?

The fearsome fight for balloon flight

1670 Italian priest Francesco de Lana hits on a nifty plan. Get some really light air from high up in the sky and fill hollow copper balls with it to lift a flying machine. So how do you get this air (that no one is sure exists)? Er, build a flying machine. And how do you do that when you haven't got the air yet...?

THAT'S WHERE MY PLAN FALLS DOWN...

1709 Brazilian priest Laurenço de Gusmão shows the King of Portugal a model hot-air balloon complete with fire. The fire spreads to the royal palace. The fire is put out, but oddly enough His Majesty isn't put out, despite nearly ending up as a roasted royal.

1755 French priest Joseph Galien (and by the way, why is it that priests were barmy about balloons?) suggested a de Lana-style flying machine 1 km long. His bosses tell him to take a nice long holiday. Now that's a holy order I could live with...

Meanwhile, a pair of brothers who weren't actually priests were about to make a brilliant, if barmy, breakthrough…

A puff of smoke

We last saw Joseph Montgolfier (1740–1810) chucking an unfortunate sheep from the top of a tower. But that was just a harmless hobby – the real business of Joe and brother Jacques (1745–1799) was making paper. I expect they were quite rich … on paper. One day in 1782, Joseph watched sparks floating up his chimney – well, there wasn't too much on telly as it hadn't been invented yet.

Joe saw that hot gases from the fire were lifting the sparks, so he decided to fill a paper bag with hot air to test whether that would rise. His landlady suggested a silk bag as it would be less likely to burn, and they watched as the bag sailed up to the ceiling. (By the way, don't go lighting fires in your house to make bags rise up – this is not a sensible thing to do, unless you'd enjoy eating prison food until you're no longer a menace to society.)

Anyway, Joe's experiments led to models that got bigger and flew higher until…

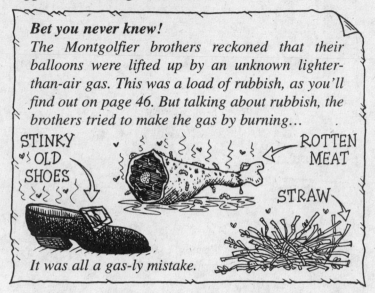

Bet you never knew!
The Montgolfier brothers reckoned that their balloons were lifted up by an unknown lighter-than-air gas. This was a load of rubbish, as you'll find out on page 46. But talking about rubbish, the brothers tried to make the gas by burning…

STINKY OLD SHOES

ROTTEN MEAT

STRAW

It was all a gas-ly mistake.

But the Montgolfiers were scenting success (and lots of other smelly things). And at last they were able to launch the first flight with an air crew in the history of the world.

AND WE'RE THE COCK-A-DOODLE-CREW!

Yes, the first living beings to fly in a flying machine were farmyard animals! And now, in a Horrible Science World Exclusive, the animals quack, bleat and crow for themselves, with a little help from King Louis XVI of France…

The King

14 September 1783 was a great day at my royal palace of Versailles. The balloon was a huge ball of blue and gold with a cage slung beneath it. I wanted to take a close look at the fire but le pong was too stinky. Pfwoar! What were they burning? Anyway, we all cheered as the balloon rose high in the sky.

The cockerel

Yes, it was a great day for us fowls - the first time we've flown without wings! Yes, it certainly was a booster for this rooster! Pity the woolly-minded sheep had to kick me as we landed in a forest 3.2 km away.

The sheep

Baah! That stupid rooster kept pecking at my legs the whole time. I'm not one to bleat, but I reckon he was scared chicken!

The duck

I'm just a duck - so what do I know? But personally I think they're all quackers. I mean, if they want to fly, why don't they just flap their wings? It works for me!

Barmy balloon quickie quiz

1 How were the Montgolfier brothers rewarded by the King?

a) They were given a cake in the shape of a balloon.

b) They were given a gold medal.

c) They were locked up in prison and forced to sniff smelly socks for making nasty whiffs in the palace.

2 How was the sheep rewarded?

a) It was made into a rather tasty mutton stew.

b) Its wool was made into an itchy pair of royal underpants.

c) It was given a home in the royal zoo.

Bet you never knew!
Scientist Jean-François Pilâtre de Rozier (1757–1785) and the Marquis d'Arlandes volunteered to fly in the Montgolfiers' balloon. The flight was a soaraway success, although they did set the balloon on fire and had to put it out using wet sponges. And they spent the flight arguing because the Marquis was too busy admiring the view to put straw on the smelly fire.

Meanwhile, French scientists were feeling mightily miffed because the balloon breakthrough had been made by a pair of papermakers and not a superb scientist. So the French Academy of Sciences asked Jacques Charles

(1746–1823) to invent a scientific flying machine. And he did – the hydrogen balloon. So what happened next? Did Charles's balloon rise to the occasion or did he go down like a lead – er – balloon?

Well, before we find out, let's look into how balloons work – it's sure to be a gas but it's nothing to sniff at! It's all to do with density…

Fearsome expressions

A scientist says…

YOU'RE TOO DENSE TO FLY…

Do you say…?

I'M QUITE BRAINY, ACTUALLY.

Answer:
Say that and the scientist really will think you're dense stupid. The scientist means your body weighs more than an equal volume of air – so it's too heavy to fly.

But here's a really cool thought…

Just imagine that your body was *less* dense than air. If your body weighed less than 5 grams, the weight of a sugar lump, you could actually float in the air! Instead of swimming pools there'd be air pools, and instead of high dives there'd be sky dives! You'd feel light-hearted as you walked on air … unless you sat on a pin and you went pop, or the gas escaped from you like a balloon with its neck open and you flew around making rude noises.

Anyway, when a balloon is full of hydrogen gas or hot air, it's less dense than the surrounding air. And that means it can rise like a bottom-burp bubble in a bath...

Here's a modern hot-air balloon...

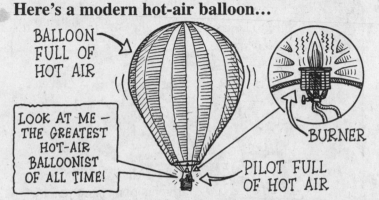

BALLOON FULL OF HOT AIR

LOOK AT ME – THE GREATEST HOT-AIR BALLOONIST OF ALL TIME!

BURNER

PILOT FULL OF HOT AIR

Air is heated by the burner. Heat gives the air molecules more energy so they travel faster and further. They push against the sides of the balloon, filling them out.

IT'S GREAT TO BE WARM!

YEAH, LET'S RUSH AROUND!

To bring the balloon down, you simply switch off the burner. The air cools and takes up less room. More cool air can enter the base of the balloon and as it becomes heavier it dips down. Simple, innit?

And now for the hydrogen balloon...

The hydrogen balloon is a bit more complicated but, as luck would have it, we're about to see one in action.

After the embarrassing near-fatal failure of their plane, Professor N Large and Wanda Wye have built a balloon. And MI Gutzache's been paid loads of money to fly it...

No, Gutzache! Hydrogen burns easily when mixed with air...

Oh dear. Is our hero a grilled Gutzache? Is Watson a hot dog? All will be revealed on page 102. But now back to Jacques Charles, who is still busily inventing the hydrogen balloon…

Bet you never knew!
A number of scientists hit on the idea of using hydrogen in a balloon before Charles, but they couldn't think of anything to put the gas in. Scottish scientist Joseph Black planned to fill a body bit from a dead calf with the gas, but he never got round to it. Maybe he was a bit of a cow-ed.

In fact, Charles's hydrogen balloon hid a silky secret…

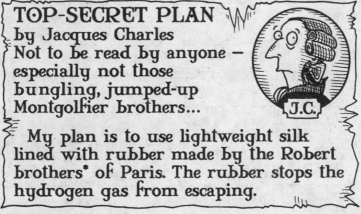

TOP-SECRET PLAN
by Jacques Charles
Not to be read by anyone – especially not those bungling, jumped-up Montgolfier brothers…

My plan is to use lightweight silk lined with rubber made by the Robert brothers* of Paris. The rubber stops the hydrogen gas from escaping.

J.C.

* Yes, more brothers!

Thousands of people turned up to see the balloon launch and the scientist put his invention under armed guard to keep the crowds away. Sadly, the guards weren't around when the unmanned balloon landed near a village and a gang of scared peasants and their dog ripped it to bits. It must have been an un-peasant surprise for the annoyed inventor.

On 12 December Charles and his friend Noel Robert took off from Paris in another balloon. An even bigger crowd came to wave them off. Overcome with emotion, Charles exclaimed...

Which was true – the trouble was the sky was also rather cold. After a flight of 43 km, Robert got out. The lightened balloon rose 2,743 metres and chilly Charles nearly froze to death. But he did get to be the first man ever to see the sun set twice in one day...

By now, all Europe was balloon barmy and what better challenge for fledgling fliers than to fly the English

Channel between France and Britain? The race was on, and by June 1784 Englishman James Sadler and Frenchman Pilâtre de Rozier were planning to make the trip. But first to start was Jean Pierre Blanchard... Now I know they didn't have radio in those days, but if they had, I bet the flight would have been broadcast live and it might have sounded like this... (Why not get a friend to read this bit aloud? You can close your eyes and imagine you were there!)

Life is full of ups and downs

Hello and welcome to Dover... My name's Mike Commentator... As I speak, brave balloonist Jean Pierre Blanchard and his passenger Dr John Jeffries are about to fly the Channel. But all is not well. We've heard that the two fliers had a row after Blanchard was caught wearing a weight-belt. The sneaky sky-sailor planned to pretend the balloon was too heavy for Jeffries – and grab all the glory for himself!

But now they've taken off! They're rising slowly – the balloon is laden with food and scientific equipment, as well as animal bladders to help it float if it lands in the sea. They've even got the world's first airmail letter...

OH NO! Blanchard's let too much gas out of the balloon. They're coming down in the sea. They're throwing things out to lighten the balloon. Out goes food, drink and scientific equipment. And now Blanchard's chucked out the useless oars and propeller he brought to control the balloon. Will the balloonists escape a ducking?

YES! They're going up – but will they make it? NO, they're coming down again! And now it looks like they're arguing! Oh my goodness, they're taking off their clothes! Yes, Blanchard's just dropped his trousers. They're down to their underwear and things are looking desperate – they've even thrown away their bottle of brandy. But they're still coming down. They're just about to hit the sea and Blanchard and Jeffries are trying to throw each other over

the side! Is it all over? NO! They're rising up again. THIS IS INCREDIBLE – they're going to make it! What a goal! Now that's what I call an up-and-under

– or is it an up-and-down-and-over? Oh no, they're coming down in a forest – they could hit the trees! Don't look at this disgusting sight – they're weeing in the bladders and dropping them over the sides. Let's hope they don't plop on any passing peasants! Well, that was a relief – they've just missed the forest. And they've landed! The crowd are going potty and the balloonists are parading about in their pants! It looks like a potty pants party! And now back to the studio!

And so the world's first airmail letter got through to Paris. But you'll be heartbroken to hear that Blanchard died of a heart attack in his balloon in 1809.

Barmy balloonists

There's something about ballooning that brings out the barmy side of the most sensible person. And as for silly people, well, they can turn barkingly barmy. The quiz you're about to tackle is based on a very barmy balloonist...

The adventures of Loopy Lunardi

The characters:

GEORGE BIGGIN — A LARGE GENTLEMAN, IN FACT A BIT OF A BIG 'UN

VINCENT'S PETS

VINCENT LUNARDI — AN ITALIAN BALLOONIST

1 Lunardi had promised to give Biggin a ride in his balloon. But the big man was too heavy. Lunardi preferred to carry his pet cat, dog and pigeon ... and what else?
a) Lots of food and wine.
b) His collection of science books.

2 During the flight everyone wanted to watch Lunardi – what was the result?
a) He killed a woman and saved a criminal's life.
b) 22,000 people visited the doctor's with stiff necks.

LET US IN, DOC – DON'T BE A PAIN IN THE NECK!

3 During the flight Lunardi's cat got cold. What did he do to help it?

a) He fed the pigeon to the cat.

b) He landed the cat in a field … and flew off.

WELL, I WOULDN'T TECHNICALLY DESCRIBE IT AS A LANDING...

MEEEOW!

Answers:

1 a) Lunardi liked his liquid lunches.

2 a) The woman was so shocked, she had a fit. The criminal was on trial, but he was set free because everyone wanted to see Lunardi fly past.

3 b) Cat lovers said Lunardi was cruel to risk the cat's life, even if it was OK to risk his own.

Bet you never knew!

The next year George Biggin and his even bigger friend Letitia Sage forced Lunardi to let them fly. Mrs Sage started scoffing Lunardi's lunch and squashed his scientific equipment with a jangling crash. A few hours later they landed in a bean field. Local children thought it was a great excuse to skip lessons, but everyone got chased by a furious farmer for trampling his beans.

GRRRR!

OOER! ERK! YIKES!

And if you think that sounds barmy, you ain't read nothing yet. French balloonists started doing really barmy publicity stunts. For example, in 1817 a Monsieur Mergot flew over Paris in a balloon … while sitting on the back of a white stag named Coco.

But balloons had a darker side – these things were DANGEROUS with a capital "D"!

Gruesome gas bags – 1

Even after Blanchard beat him to it, Pilâtre de Rozier still wanted to fly the Channel. Trouble is, he wanted to do it in a combined hot-air and hydrogen balloon – and remember what happens when you mix fire and hydrogen? When the balloon burst into flames, the scientist and his co-pilot were the first people to die in an air crash. And in honour of the event the bloody scene was painted for some rather sick souvenirs. Sick bags, anyone?

Gruesome gas bags – 2

Meanwhile, other scientists were dreaming of taking a balloon as high as they could to find out how the air changed with height. But this turned out to be *incredibly* dangerous. Read on, this next bit's a "height" for sore eyes…

Fearsome flight fact file

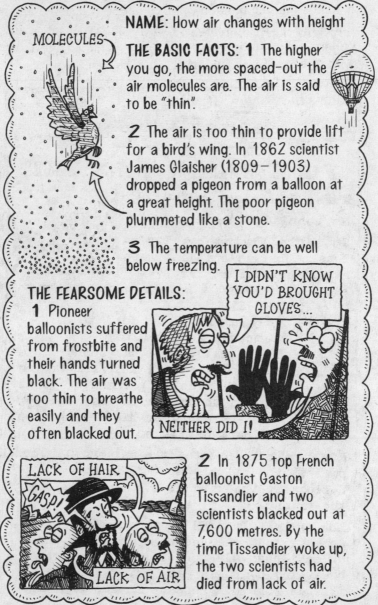

MOLECULES

NAME: How air changes with height

THE BASIC FACTS: 1 The higher you go, the more spaced-out the air molecules are. The air is said to be "thin".

2 The air is too thin to provide lift for a bird's wing. In 1862 scientist James Glaisher (1809–1903) dropped a pigeon from a balloon at a great height. The poor pigeon plummeted like a stone.

3 The temperature can be well below freezing.

THE FEARSOME DETAILS:
1 Pioneer balloonists suffered from frostbite and their hands turned black. The air was too thin to breathe easily and they often blacked out.

I DIDN'T KNOW YOU'D BROUGHT GLOVES...

NEITHER DID I!

LACK OF HAIR

GASP!

LACK OF AIR

2 In 1875 top French balloonist Gaston Tissandier and two scientists blacked out at 7,600 metres. By the time Tissandier woke up, the two scientists had died from lack of air.

Another danger with taking a hydrogen balloon to a great height is that the balloon can explode. Because the air is thinner, the air pressure is weaker on the sides of the balloon. This allows the hydrogen inside to push out with greater force and burst the balloon. And that's what happened to this fearless flier…

FAMOUS FEARLESS FLIER FILES

Name: John Wise (1808–1879)

Nationality: American

Got into flying by: Trying lots of horrible flight experiments. For example:

- He tied a kitten to a kite and flew it.
- He dropped a cat tied to a parachute from a window.

The animals lived but John's neighbours banned him from trying any more cruel experiments, so he decided to make a hot-air balloon. But it crashed on his neighbour's roof and set it on fire.

High point: Invented the rip panel. You pull it to let the gas out of your balloon if the wind is blowing it along the ground.

Low point: In 1859 he was flying with some friends when he went to sleep under a leaky gas valve. He nearly died from breathing hydrogen gas, but luckily his friends woke him because he was snoring.

Most dangerous moment: In 1838 his balloon burst at 4,000 metres. Luckily Wise had wisely packed a parachute.

Deadly death details: In 1879 Wise made his 463rd balloon flight. The balloon was flimsy and Wise thought it might be dangerous. He was prepared to risk his own neck, but he asked the young man who was about fly with him to stay behind. The man didn't listen. The balloon crashed into Lake Michigan and both men died.

YOU SHOULDN'T HAVE COME...

NO, IT WASN'T WISE, WISE!

Got the message? Balloons are horribly hard to fly and easy to crash, and even today they're only safe in the hands of experts. But in the 1850s, flight fans thought they'd invented a superb solution...

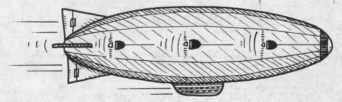

ARRGGGGH! Am I seeing things or did a huge cigar-shaped balloon just drift across the page? Oh well, you'd best read on. Reading is believing...

AWESOME AIRSHIPS

WOW, that really *was* an airship! An airship is a giant balloon that you can steer – so let's steer our way through this crazy chapter and check out their stunning secrets…

Fearsome flight fact file

NAME: Airships

THE BASIC FACTS: **1** An airship is made from several gas bags inside a tough wooden or metal skeleton. The outside of the ship is protected by a fabric or metal skin.

2 The craft is powered by engines and propellers, and steered by rudders.

3 The pointy shape of the airship enables it to move with less drag than a balloon.

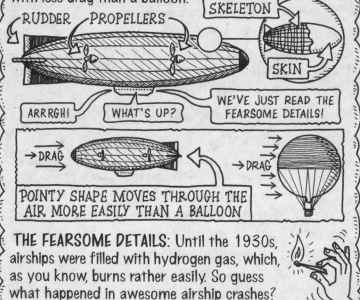

RUDDER PROPELLERS SKELETON SKIN

ARRRGH! WHAT'S UP?

WE'VE JUST READ THE FEARSOME DETAILS!

→ DRAG → DRAG

POINTY SHAPE MOVES THROUGH THE AIR MORE EASILY THAN A BALLOON

THE FEARSOME DETAILS: Until the 1930s, airships were filled with hydrogen gas, which, as you know, burns rather easily. So guess what happened in awesome airship crashes?

The fearsome fight for airship flight

1852 Frenchman Henri Gifford (1825–1882) adds a small engine to a cigar-shaped balloon. The engine is too weak to power the balloon and the craft gets blown backwards.

1883 Gaston Tissandier (remember him from page 57?) and his brother Albert experiment with a 4.8 km per hour motor. The airship flies as fast as a granny shuffles to the shops. Well, almost.

1898 Brazilian genius Albert Santos-Dumont builds his first airship and learns how to fly it. Awesome Albert is so immensely interesting that you can read all about him on page 62.

1900 Retired General Ferdinand von Zeppelin (1838–1917) builds his first airship or zeppelin. (I wonder where the name came from?)

1915 Zeppelins bomb Britain in the First World War. The Brits panic until they realize the big slow zeppelins are easy to shoot down. And then the Germans' panic and stop zeppelin raids.

1924 A zeppelin flies the Atlantic. In the 1930s zeppelins are the poshest way to travel the world.

1930 The British airship R101 crashes, killing 48 people. The Brits give up on airships.

1937 The *Hindenburg*, the biggest zeppelin ever built, crashes in the USA. Suddenly the balloon bubble bursts for airships.

So airships were as dangerous as a dinner date with a dinosaur, and one man who knew this more than most was Albert Santos-Dumont. Let's go and meet him right now…

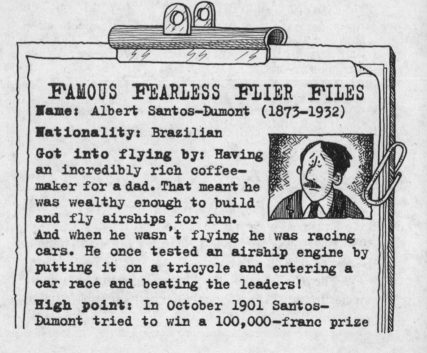

FAMOUS FEARLESS FLIER FILES

Name: Albert Santos-Dumont (1873–1932)

Nationality: Brazilian

Got into flying by: Having an incredibly rich coffee-maker for a dad. That meant he was wealthy enough to build and fly airships for fun.

And when he wasn't flying he was racing cars. He once tested an airship engine by putting it on a tricycle and entering a car race and beating the leaders!

High point: In October 1901 Santos-Dumont tried to win a 100,000-franc prize

for flying from St Cloud on the outskirts
of Paris, rounding the Eiffel Tower and
returning to St Cloud in half an hour. He
did it with seconds to spare.

"Have I won the prize?" Santos-Dumont
called.

YES! YES! YES!

roared the crazy, cheering crowd.

"No", muttered a grumpy judge from the
Paris Aero Club. The fearless flier hadn't
lowered his guide rope in time. At this
point the rich businessman who had
offered the prize said that he had won —
it was either that or face a riot. Albert
gave the money away to the poor.

Low point: Following his triumph, Santos-
Dumont toured Britain and the USA, but
his airships were damaged by vandals.

Most dangerous moment: In his bid to
win the prize, Santos-Dumont suffered
many hair-raising crashes. For example
his first airship folded over in mid-air.
He said later...

FOR A MOMENT I WAS IN
THE PRESENCE OF DEATH

But just as the craft crashed downwards,
he saw two boys flying a kite. The
falling flier shouted to them to grab his
airship guide rope and run with it
against the wind. The ship gained some
lift from the wind and made a soft landing.

Deadly death details: Oddly enough Santos-
Dumont wasn't killed in a crash — but be
warned, it's NOT a happy ending! Make sure
you've got a box of paper hankies handy...

63

Awesome Albert's downfall

In the 1900s Albert Santos-Dumont was the most famous flier in the world. Well, come to think of it, he was the ONLY flier in the world.

In fact he even helped the first-ever child to fly in a powered flying machine. One day in 1903 the brave Brazilian landed in a children's fair. All the kids begged for a ride and all their spoil-sport parents said...

But seven-year-old Clarkson Potter pestered his parents so hard they gave in. In the end, though, he only went up a few metres.

But after planes became popular Albert didn't do so well. Although he was the first person to fly a powered plane in Europe, his planes always seemed to crash. As he grew older many people thought he was mad. He spent time in mental hospitals and dreamt of making a pair of wings and flying from a window. Quite unfairly, he blamed himself for the way planes had been used to kill people in war. One day Santos-Dumont was staying in a hotel in Sao Paolo, Brazil. Civil war was raging and the ageing flier spotted a plane dropping bombs.

"What have I done?" he muttered.

He went up to his room and took his own life.

Zero hour for the zeppelins

By the time Santos-Dumont died, a lot had changed in the floating world of airships. Zeppelins were the world's number-one airships but things were about to go fearsomely wrong…

HORRIBLE HOLIDAYS PRESENT

Come fly on the Hindenburg!

It's got everything you've ever wanted and a lot of things you don't.

Your very own cabin.

Hot and cold water.

Air conditioning.

It's a gas!

Library, lounge (complete with piano) and bar.

On-board pastry chef bakes fresh buns every day!

Guaranteed smooth flight so you can munch your buns and enjoy the view with none of that nasty air sickness.

THE SMALL PRINT

The hydrogen gas and chemicals used to stiffen the fabric sides of the craft have turned the Hindenburg into a flying bomb. Have you written your will yet?

OOER!

On 6 May 1937 the *Hindenburg* was just coming into dock at Lakehurst, New Jersey... Suddenly a flame appeared that rapidly swallowed up the ship. The great airship crashed to the ground amid the screams of its unlucky passengers. Forty people died, the *Hindenburg* was destroyed ... and it all took just 34 seconds.

That was bad enough. But a cine-camera recorded the explosive event and a local radio reporter recorded it. The world got the message – airships were awesomely unsafe.

But were they? Even in 1937 it was possible to use the safer gas helium instead of hydrogen. Airships needn't burn. What killed off the airship in the end wasn't safety fears – it was the success of a nippy little rival with two wings and a whizzy propeller. And in the next chapter we'll find out how it got off the ground... Get ready to spin that propeller!

THE WRIGHT WAY TO INVENT THE PLANE

So how does anyone invent the plane? Well there's a bit more to it than sitting on the toilet and getting inspired and shouting "Eureka!" In fact, inventing is HARDER than chewing a concrete toffee. In this cruel chapter we'll find out why the Wright brothers got it Wright and why nearly everyone else ended up grumpy, wet … or dead.

Fearsome flying flops

Back in Victorian times lots of inventors dreamt of making a flying machine. Trouble is, most of them had little idea of the forces that affect flight, and their planes were as useless as a giraffe with a sore throat. But that won't stop Honest Bob trying to sell you one. YOU HAVE BEEN WARNED!

HONEST BOB'S PLANE PRODUCTS PRESENTS...

"My Bob's really musical. When he was little he was always on the fiddle." Bob's mum

HERE ARE SOME CLASSIC PLANES YOU'LL BE FLYING TO DIE, I MEAN, DYING TO FLY...

I Fancy a trip to Beijing? Henson and Stringfellow's steam-powered plane will get you there! Finest 1840s technology!

Only £99,999.05p – but I'll knock off the 5p for cash.

ARE WE REALLY FLYING?

NO, IT'S JUST AN ADVERT!

2 You'll be batty not to buy this bat-winged plane (1890) by Clement Ader. People say it's an objet d'art — although it looks more like a paper dart to me.

Only £150,000 plus a few hidden extras.

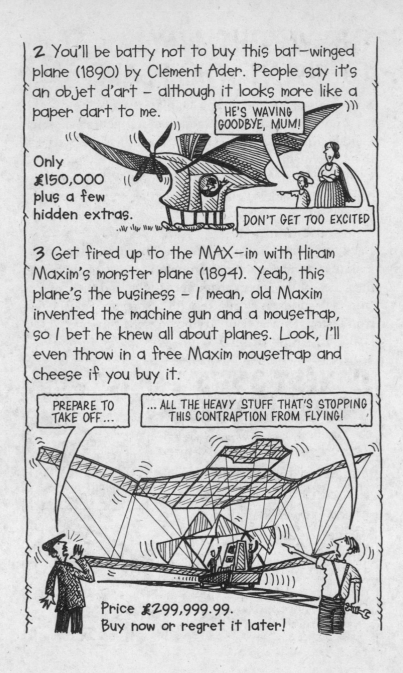

HE'S WAVING GOODBYE, MUM!

DON'T GET TOO EXCITED

3 Get fired up to the MAX-im with Hiram Maxim's monster plane (1894). Yeah, this plane's the business — I mean, old Maxim invented the machine gun and a mousetrap, so I bet he knew all about planes. Look, I'll even throw in a free Maxim mousetrap and cheese if you buy it.

PREPARE TO TAKE OFF...

... ALL THE HEAVY STUFF THAT'S STOPPING THIS CONTRAPTION FROM FLYING!

Price £299,999.99. Buy now or regret it later!

4 You'll be Venetian blind not to buy it! (Well, it looks like a Venetian blind!) Horatio Phillips's multi-wingy thingie (1904). I mean, talk about character – this plane's got it in spades. If it doesn't take off, you can always put it in your window and it'll keep the sun out.

Price £199,999. Unless I'm in a good mood – then it's £299,999.

STILL ON THE GROUND

OH WELL, I'LL USE IT AS A CAR!

A few facts that Bob was going to tell you some day…
1 The designers thought plane 1 would fly to China, but it was too heavy to fly at all.
2 Plane 2 hopped in 1890, but that was all.
3 Plane 3 hopped slightly in the air and broke the rail it was running on.
4 According to its inventor, plane 4 hopped 152 metres – yeah, right. Mind you, old Horatio was one of the first people to realize the importance of aerofoil wings. He just made rather too many of them…

Meanwhile, other flight fans were being a little more thoughtful. They wanted to understand about flight before trying to build a plane, so they studied birds, and built and flew gliders and learnt to fly them. These people included the Wright brothers, but before we pay them a visit we really ought to glide over a few facts…

Fearsome flight fact file

NAME: Gliders

THE BASIC FACTS: **1** Gliders are towed into the air and their wings produce enough lift to fly. Gliders have long wings to pick up as much lift as they can.

THAT'S HIGH ENOUGH – PASS ME THE SCISSORS!

2 Gliders gradually glide down to earth but they can stay up longer if they find a rising column of hot air called a thermal. Thermals rise from hot rocks or tarmac.

HOW'S IT GOING?

THERMALS

I'M GETTING THE HANG OF IT!

3 A hang-glider is a one-person glider with an A-shaped wing.

THE FEARSOME DETAILS: Two leading glider pioneers – Otto Lilienthal and Percy Pilcher – met fearsome fates. Crash on to pages 76 and 78 if you want to read the deadly details.

Not surprisingly, the cleverest bloke in this book was keen to study how birds flew. And that's how he came to build the world's first glider…

Hall of fame: Sir George Cayley (1771–1857) Nationality: British
Young George was just 12 years old when he heard about the Montgolfier brothers' amazing balloon, and he

became flight-mad. He started making his own hot-air balloons powered by candles (very dangerous, so don't try it). And then he experimented with model helicopters made of feathers. As he liked to boast…

I HAVE IDEAS, LOTS OF IDEAS THAT MAY BE MADE TO WORK.

And so he had! In a lifetime of spare-time study (he was a busy landowner and politician), Cayley worked out…

• The ideal shape for a plane.
• The ideal shape for a wing.
• The importance of the forces of lift and thrust.
• The sort of controls a plane would need.

Here's an experiment which shows clever Cayley at his best. Eager to find out the angle of a wing that gives the most lift, he made a model wing based on the wing of a dead crow. He spun the model on a whirling arm powered by a weight that he dropped downstairs and found that an angle of 45° was best. Now that's what I call a stair-lift. By the way, cunning Cayley had to weight, er wait, for his wife to be away as she didn't approve of him experimenting in the house.

And here's how Cayley built his glider…
Cayley built his first model glider in 1799 and flew it as a kite – but he didn't get round to building a full-sized glider for ten years, and he didn't test one with a human on board for another *thirty* years! As I said, George was *very* busy.

In 1849 Cayley finally tested his glider with a person on board. That person was a ten-year-old boy and he flew a few metres. The boy was the first person to have flown in a glider and you might think the lucky lad became incredibly famous and sold his story to the newspapers for pots of money. But no – science is horribly unfair and no one even noted the boy's name!

Four years later, Cayley built a machine that could carry an adult. Once again there are few records of this world-shattering event, but Cayley's ten-year-old granddaughter saw the whole thing and here's how she might have described it...

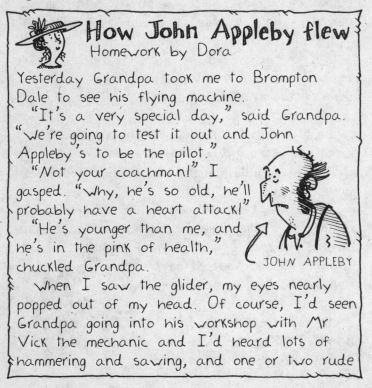

How John Appleby flew
Homework by Dora

Yesterday Grandpa took me to Brompton Dale to see his flying machine.

"It's a very special day," said Grandpa. "We're going to test it out and John Appleby's to be the pilot."

"Not your coachman!" I gasped. "Why, he's so old, he'll probably have a heart attack!"

"He's younger than me, and he's in the pink of health," chuckled Grandpa.

JOHN APPLEBY

When I saw the glider, my eyes nearly popped out of my head. Of course, I'd seen Grandpa going into his workshop with Mr Vick the mechanic and I'd heard lots of hammering and sawing, and one or two rude words when they hammered their fingers. But I'd never dreamt of anything like this...

downhill

Proudly Grandpa showed off his creation. He pointed out the rudder at the rear to help Mr Appleby steer the craft and the elevators on the wings to help it go higher.

"All my own inventions," Grandpa beamed.

By now a crowd of villagers had gathered to watch the takeoff and some of the men offered to pull the rope on the front of the craft to get it going.

John Appleby was sitting in the craft, wearing his warmest coat - but I noticed he didn't look quite as jolly and red-faced as usual.

"You'll be fine, Appleby," smiled Grandpa, cheerfully slapping his coachman on the back.

John Appleby gulped and nodded. I bet he was thinking what would happen if the glider crashed and he broke all his bones and his brains came out of his ears.

SPLURB!

With a signal from Grandpa, the men started pulling on the ropes. Harder and harder they pulled. The glider slid over the grass and bounced downhill and then...

Everyone gasped as it took off. It flew like a paper dart over the stream and across the valley and... OH NO! It bashed into the other side of the valley in a big cloud of dust. I felt disappointed - I thought Grandpa's glider would fly much further. Everyone rushed over to see if John Appleby was all right. Was he dead?

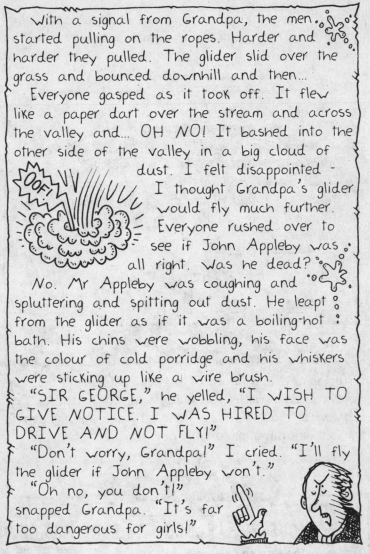

No. Mr Appleby was coughing and spluttering and spitting out dust. He leapt from the glider as if it was a boiling-hot bath. His chins were wobbling, his face was the colour of cold porridge and his whiskers were sticking up like a wire brush.

"SIR GEORGE," he yelled, "I WISH TO GIVE NOTICE. I WAS HIRED TO DRIVE AND NOT FLY!"

"Don't worry, Grandpa!" I cried. "I'll fly the glider if John Appleby won't."

"Oh no, you don't!" snapped Grandpa. "It's far too dangerous for girls!"

"Oh well," I hear you remark, "at least John Appleby became world-famous..." But he didn't. In fact, the newspapers didn't even report the story. Most people thought that making a plane was impossible and they couldn't see the point of Sir George's experiments. You see, no one had invented an engine that was light and powerful enough to get a plane in the air.

Bet you never knew!
1 The steam-powered engines of Cayley's day were very heavy and needed boilers to make steam. Not to mention a supply of water to boil and coal to burn.
2 Cayley realized this made it impossible for a plane to fly and planned to build a gunpowder-powered engine ... before he realized it was too dangerous.

MAYBE NOT!

So, for now, the future of flight depended on building better gliders and that's exactly what flying freaks tried to do. The most famous of them all was a German genius who didn't mind making the odd sacrifice...

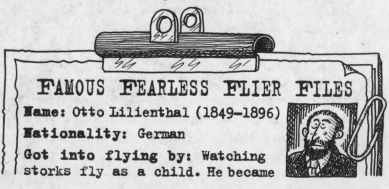

FAMOUS FEARLESS FLIER FILES
Name: Otto Lilienthal (1849–1896)
Nationality: German
Got into flying by: Watching storks fly as a child. He became

an engineer but he retired to build gliders.

High point: Gliding several hundred metres at heights of 30 metres. Lilienthal was the first human in history to glide like a bird and he made 2,000 glides — some from a specially built hill. Today the modern sport of hang-gliding is inspired by his work.

WEEEEEE!

Low point: Trying to build a flying machine with flapping wings. Experts say it wouldn't have got off the ground.

Most dangerous moment: Just about every moment he was in the air. Lilienthal's gliders were built out of wood and fabric, and they were hard to control in windy weather. To change course, he had to swing his body from side to side.

Deadly death details: Luckless Lil was trying to turn in a wind. He fell and broke his back and his final words were, "Sacrifices must be made." In other words, he was dying for flying.

Oddly enough, Lilienthal's famous fate did nothing to put people off gliding. It even seemed to encourage them!

Bet you never knew!
The US champion gliding geek was another ex-engineer named Octave Chanute (1832–1910). Chanute was a little too old to fly so he asked a man named Augustus Herring to test his gliders. (When the glider didn't work too well, I bet he lost his temper and turned into a red Herring.)

In Britain, Lilienthal's lead was taken up by Percy Pilcher (1867–1899). Percy had worked for Hiram Maxim (remember him from page 68?), but he became a fan of Lilienthal and even flew with his hero. And, like Lilienthal, he was to die in a glider crash.

FLYING NEWS
1899

PERCY PILCHER PERISHES!

Flying freak Percy Pilcher perished after a gliding glitch caused a cruel crash. Penniless Percy invited some bigwigs to watch the takeoff of his new powered plane. But bad weather and engine trouble caused his hopes to take a nosedive. Plucky Percy decided to show off his glider even though it was soaked by the rain. The glider fell to bits and Percy's fall proved fully fatal.

CRUNCH!

Bet you never knew!
Experts think that, with a couple of tweaks, Percy's plane might have flown. So thanks to a spot of engine bother and rotten weather, Percy missed out on flying the world's first powered plane. Sadly, instead of tasting the high life he ended up biting the dust.

And talking about powered planes, it's time for some very exciting news for anyone who gets excited by engines…

Exciting engine news

The reason why Percy could build a powered plane was that a new kind of engine had been developed. Let's face the facts – this new engine was vital for the fearsome future of flight...

Fearsome flight fact file

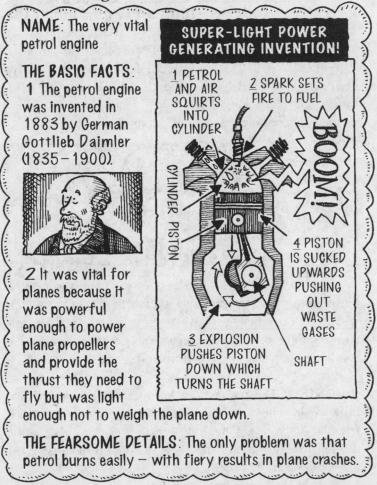

NAME: The very vital petrol engine

THE BASIC FACTS:
1 The petrol engine was invented in 1883 by German Gottlieb Daimler (1835–1900).

2 It was vital for planes because it was powerful enough to power plane propellers and provide the thrust they need to fly but was light enough not to weigh the plane down.

SUPER-LIGHT POWER GENERATING INVENTION!

1 PETROL AND AIR SQUIRTS INTO CYLINDER

2 SPARK SETS FIRE TO FUEL

BOOM!

CYLINDER

PISTON

4 PISTON IS SUCKED UPWARDS PUSHING OUT WASTE GASES

3 EXPLOSION PUSHES PISTON DOWN WHICH TURNS THE SHAFT

SHAFT

THE FEARSOME DETAILS: The only problem was that petrol burns easily – with fiery results in plane crashes.

And it was the petrol engine that made it possible for a pair of bicycle mechanics from Ohio, USA, to make the world's first-ever powered flight. Back in 1899 no one had ever heard of them (except maybe their mum), but armed with a few bike spares, cloth and some bits of wood they would change the history of the world…

Everything you ever wanted to know about the Wright brothers

When Orville Wright (1871–1948) and his brother Wilbur (1867–1912) were little, their dad gave them a toy helicopter powered by a rubber band. They loved it so much they broke it. They built a new one but their grumpy, spoilsport teacher took it away.

Just think about it! That teacher set back the tide of human progress by years and it's worth sharing this idea with your teacher next time they seize your pocket computer game. And you can always get your revenge by torturing them with this terrible test…

WARNING! These questions are rated really hard, if not impossible. They are only suitable for teachers and NOT friends. If you are feeling kind, you can give your teacher the right to ask the class to vote on the answer to ONE question.

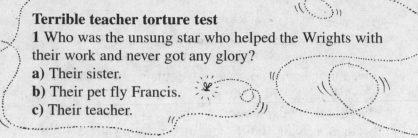

Terrible teacher torture test

1 Who was the unsung star who helped the Wrights with their work and never got any glory?
a) Their sister.
b) Their pet fly Francis.
c) Their teacher.

2 What did Wilbur and Orville do as a hobby?
a) They printed a newspaper.
b) They entered custard-pie throwing competitions.
c) They gave lessons to local children.

3 What did Wilbur do when a boy sat on his best hat?
a) He made the boy test a dangerous glider.
b) Nothing at all.
c) He gave the boy loads of horribly hard homework.

I WOULDN'T HAVE MINDED... BUT I WAS WEARING IT!

4 The Wrights tried to fly at Kill Devil Sandhill near Kitty Hawk, North Carolina. Why?
a) The sand gave them a nice soft landing when they crashed.
b) The wind blows all the time.
c) Their old teacher lived there.

5 Where did a bit of the Wrights' plane end up?
a) Holding up their mum's washing line.
b) The moon.
c) On display at their old school.

THIS IS ONE SMALL STEP FOR MAN... HANG ON, WHAT'S THIS?

Answers:

1 a) So let's hear three cheers for Katharine Wright, who ran the bike business when the boys were off inventing the plane. She gave them the cash they needed to get off the ground.

2 a) But the really interesting thing is that the inventive brothers actually built their own printing press from an old tombstone and the top of a pram (plus other bits 'n' pieces).

3 b) This story shows how patient Wilbur was. You could try to explain that patience with children is a sign of genius – but would your teacher be patient enough to listen?

4 Ha ha – trick question. The answer is **a)** AND **b)** and your teacher can't have a point unless they said both. In fact the wind wasn't as constant as the brothers hoped, and millions of mosquitoes sucked their blood. But at least there was no one around to spy on them and pinch their ideas. (The Wrights were keen to keep their invention a secret until they could make money from it.)

5 b) When the Apollo 11 astronauts landed on the moon in 1969 there was a bit of the Wrights' plane in their spacecraft. Well, you didn't think it flew there on its own, did you?

What your teacher's score means...

5 CHEAT! Clearly this person is unfit to be a teacher!

3–4 Good. Make sure the questions are harder next time.

0–2 Poor. Make your teacher write out 1,000 times "I really ought to know more about the Wright brothers" while you take the day off.

By the way, the c) answers were to do with school, so if your teacher's answers were all c) they are clearly overworked and deserve a long holiday. And you'll have to take one too!

The Wrights get busy...

From 1899 onwards the Wright brothers spent all their spare time building and testing gliders and planes until they had built a plane that could fly. And that's not all...

• They invented a lighter and more powerful petrol engine.

• Plus a new, more powerful propeller.

• They built a wind tunnel (that's a machine in which air is blown through a box) to work out which aerofoil wing shape gave the most lift.

• But, best of all, they realized that it wasn't enough to build a plane. They had to be able to control it in the air. And so they invented wing-warping, which means flexing the wings to alter the amount of lift they provide. By doing this the Wrights could tilt and turn the plane in mid-air.

And they did all this by trial and error – testing, testing and testing their designs until they worked. In all, they tested...

• Hundreds of aerofoil shapes in their wind tunnel.

• Their third glider nearly 1,000 times.

Although they didn't know it at the time, the Wrights were in a race to invent the plane. And their rival was scenting success. His name was Samuel P Langley (1834–1906) and he was an astronomer who got hooked on flying after going to a scientific talk. Now I could tell you more about Langley, but it so happens he's coming back from the dead to tell you himself. He's on the TV show that digs the dirt to unearth its guests...

And what's more, we're getting ahead of our story. After all, back in 1903, when Langley's plane flopped in the river, the Wrights' plane, the *Flyer*, wasn't a flyer. It hadn't even got off the ground.

And to tell the story of what happened, let's peek at Orville Wright's secret diary. Er, I bought it from Honest Bob, so it *might* be a forgery.

Orville Wright's Secret Diary

December 16 1903, Kitty Hawk, North Carolina. It's all my brother's fault. Two days ago he tried to take off but the controls were set wrong and he crashed. Ever since, we have been repairing the damage and waiting for the wind to drop so we can risk trying to fly again. Time is running out and we've got to be home for Christmas or Pa will never forgive us!

GRR, WHERE ARE THEY?

December 17 1903
We decided to fly this morning. To be honest, there's been times when I've doubted we'd do it. It's taken four years of hard work. Would it all be worth it? I wondered. I asked a local named John Daniels to take a photo if the plane flew - but John hadn't used a camera and he didn't know which end was which. Slowly, we pushed the plane from its shed. John and his friends helped.

CAN I GO FIRST, BRUV?

NO WAY!

I lay on the lower wing (that's where the pilot has to go - we really ought to invent a comfy seat!). As Wilbur swung the propeller to start the engine, the others pushed the plane along our home-made rails. The engine coughed and spluttered into life... WHOOSH! My heart jumped into my mouth. I was up in the air. I WAS FLYING! At last the plane came down but I'd done it. The flight was awesome, it was MASSIVE, it was all of 40 metres - and I must have been in the air for a WHOLE 12 SECONDS. WOW!

I CAN DO BETTER THAN THAT!

And it just got better. John Daniels did manage to take my photo - pity I wasn't smiling at the time! And after coffee Wilbur flew 52 metres - huh, trust my brother to try to beat me! So I showed him - I flew 61 metres, although I did go up and down a bit. But just when I felt like crowing, my big-headed brother flew 100 metres, although he did crash. Luckily he's fine - what's with him always crashing? Then it was my go and I beat his record, but then he flew for nearly a minute and got 260 metres. Show-off! We sent a telegram to Pa telling him we'd be home for Christmas. Now that's what I call a GOOD day's work!

ANYBODY WANT A WING?

And so, after years of trying, humans were flying powered planes. But many people thought it was no big deal. After all, the Wrights had flown for less than a minute and the only papers that reported the event got it all wrong and said Wilbur ran around shouting "Eureka!"

But from now on the fearsome fight wasn't to fly. It was to fly *better*! And the race was on to build better planes…

88

PLANE-CRAZY PLANES

This is a chapter about machines. Flying machines and not-so-flying machines. It's got the sort of machines that you wouldn't send your worst teacher up in, and it's even got helicopters too. So, if you're all aboard, let's take to the air…

Now I bet you're itching to find out what happened to the Wright brothers, who were last seen celebrating their success with a slap-up Christmas dinner. The Wrights knew they had to improve their plane before they could think of selling it and making money. So they built not one but two planes, *Flyers* 2 and 3. And they tested the planes until they could…

- Fly 66 km.
- Reach the dizzy height of 110 metres.

At last, in 1908, the brothers set out to wow the world and sell planes. Orville went to Washington to wow the US army. And Wilbur went to Paris to wow European flying fans.

At first the French didn't think much of Wilbur. They didn't like his greasy old clothes and the way he slept in a plane shed and ate from tins and burped in public. But once they saw what his plane could do, they changed their tune…

After all, the best the Europeans could manage was a giant box-kite, which our old pal Santos-Dumont managed to hop 4.5 metres off the ground: not even as far as Wilbur's best 1903 effort.

So when the Europeans saw Wilbur flying happily across country and changing course in mid-air, they were gobsmacked. They rushed to their own garden sheds and started knocking up all kinds of crazy craft based on the Wrights' planes. But tragedy was just around the corner...

The Wrights' planes were FEARSOMELY dangerous fliers:
• They had NO brakes.
• No undercarriage wheels.
• No safely belt.
• The only way women could fly in them was with their legs tied together so their dresses wouldn't blow over their heads.

In 1908 Orville was flying over a cemetery in Washington when he lost control. He was badly hurt and his passenger Thomas Selfridge was killed. The aeroplane had claimed its first victim…

Bet you never knew!
1 Despite the safety problems, the Wrights made plane-loads of money from selling their planes. But they hated other pilots stealing their ideas and they spent years in the courts fighting their rivals. Wilbur ruined his health with worry. In 1912 he died of a grisly gut disease.
2 The Europeans didn't copy everything from the Wrights. They began to use wing flaps called ailerons (a-ler-rons) instead of wing warping. Ailerons proved ideal for tilting wings to turn a plane in mid-air (see page 104 for the full flap facts).

But talking about dangerous machines … here's Honest Bob with a collection of perilous planes. Yes, they're more dangerous than a tiger with toothache, so which one would you fancy for your death-day, er, birthday?

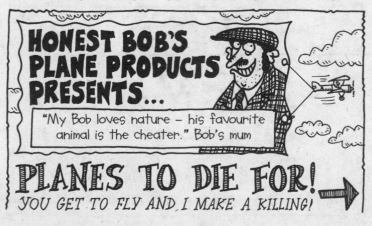

HONEST BOB'S PLANE PRODUCTS PRESENTS...

"My Bob loves nature – his favourite animal is the cheater." Bob's mum

PLANES TO DIE FOR!
YOU GET TO FLY AND I MAKE A KILLING!

1 The Christmas Bullet (1918) This ye olde antique plane was designed by Dr William Christmas, so it makes an ideal Christmas present. Dr C was a medical doc and I bet that came in handy when his plane crashed. It goes like a bullet and it's twice as deadly. (Oops, I'm getting a bit too honest!) Price – it's only £999,999.99.

ERK... I'LL BE IN A WOODEN BOX BY BOXING DAY!

2 The Mayfly (1910) Built in Ireland by Lilian Bland, the Mayfly is held together with piano wire. A must for music lovers! The engine was made from Lil's aunt's ear trumpet and an old whisky bottle.

WHEN THEY ASKED ME, I SAID, "IT **MAY FLY** ... AND IT MAY NOT!"

Price – it's yours for 50p (plus £654,321 postage and packing).

3 Le Grand (1913) What a grand way to fly! You get a crew of three – one person to fly the plane, one to sit at the front and tell the pilot what they see, and one to walk backwards and forwards to balance the plane. Relax on the supplied-as-standard comfy four armchairs and sofa! Price – you can't put a price on this kind of luxury but I'll try – it's £2,222,222.22.

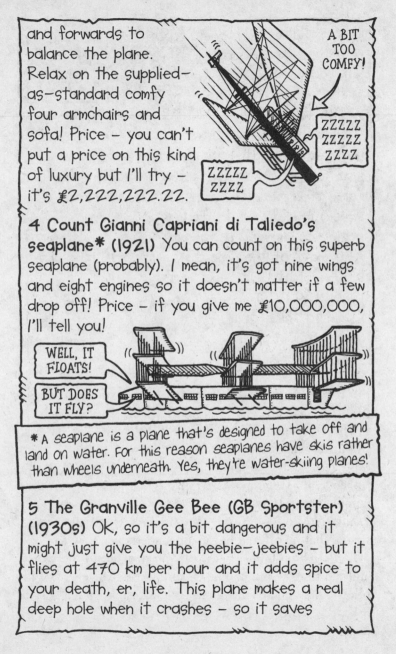

A BIT TOO COMFY!

ZZZZZ ZZZZZ ZZZZ

ZZZZZ ZZZZ

4 Count Gianni Capriani di Taliedo's seaplane* (1921)

You can count on this superb seaplane (probably). I mean, it's got nine wings and eight engines so it doesn't matter if a few drop off! Price – if you give me £10,000,000, I'll tell you!

WELL, IT FLOATS!

BUT DOES IT FLY?

* A seaplane is a plane that's designed to take off and land on water. For this reason seaplanes have skis rather than wheels underneath. Yes, they're water-skiing planes!

5 The Granville Gee Bee (GB Sportster) (1930s)

OK, so it's a bit dangerous and it might just give you the heebie-jeebies – but it flies at 470 km per hour and it adds spice to your death, er, life. This plane makes a real deep hole when it crashes – so it saves getting buried! Price – name your price, and I'll just add £456,789!

... BETTER HEAD FOR THAT GRAVEYARD

6 The Flying Flea (Pou de Ciel) (1930s)

Supplied as a kit – you build this plane yourself in your shed. Yeah, it's ideal for DIE fans, er, I mean DIY fans. It's cheap and cheerful, and it even flies upside down. Well, it does that most of the time.

Price – just 50p.
Glue: £89,000.
Come to think of it, you can just fly it away – if you dare!

YIKES! I'VE BEEN ITCHING TO FLY ONE BUT IT'S NOT UP TO SCRATCH!

Six things Honest Bob forgot to tell you about these planes

1 The Christmas Bullet was a killer craft. On its first flight, its wings fell off and its pilot was killed. On the third test flight, another pilot died. Dr C was a flying fibber who stole many of his inventions from other companies.

2 Lilian's Mayfly didn't fly – it hopped. Her uncle was so scared that he offered her a car if she never flew again.

3 In 1913 Le Grand was the biggest plane in the world and the first with a cabin. Despite, or because of, all its pilots, the plane designed by Russian genius Igor Sikorsky (1889–1972) actually flew!

94

4 The good news – this plane took off from Lake Meggidore. The bad news – its middle wings fell off and it crashed. Everyone had a good laugh … except the plane-ly annoyed Count.

5 The Gee Bee was built for racing and actually set a speed record. It also had a nasty habit of killing its pilots. Two Gee Bees crashed and killed their pilots. So the makers put bits of the two downed planes together to make a third Gee Bee – which crashed and killed its pilot. For some reason this put people off flying it.

6 In the 1930s there was a craze in France, Britain and the USA for these home-built planes designed by Henri Mignet. Mad Mignet had been plane-crazy since he built a glider that landed on his little sister. He said:

IF YOU CAN NAIL TOGETHER A PACKING CRATE YOU CAN CONSTRUCT AN AEROPLANE

Trouble was, when the Flea flopped upside down, you couldn't get it the right way up until you crashed and died (probably).

An important announcement by the author…

So far, all the planes in this chapter have been dismal embarrassing flops, but there *were* good planes in the 1920s and 1930s… Between 1919 and 1931 the Schneider Trophy seaplane races encouraged designers in the USA, Germany, Italy, Britain and France to build faster planes. The designs inspired fighter planes, like the British Spitfire and the Italian Maachi C200.

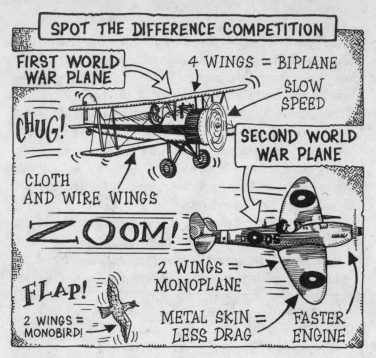

SPOT THE DIFFERENCE COMPETITION

FIRST WORLD WAR PLANE

4 WINGS = BIPLANE

SLOW SPEED

CHUG!

SECOND WORLD WAR PLANE

CLOTH AND WIRE WINGS

ZOOM!

FLAP!

2 WINGS = MONOBIRD!

2 WINGS = MONOPLANE

METAL SKIN = LESS DRAG

FASTER ENGINE

Horrible helicopters

And that wasn't all. In the 1930s designers were working on a totally new type of flying machine. A machine that took off and hovered without bother. Or at least it was supposed to…

Five facts that your teacher probably doesn't know about helicopters

1 The helicopter was invented in ancient China. Or at least a toy helicopter that whizzed up in the air when you pulled a string was invented there. It reached Europe in the Middle Ages.

2 Before 1900 loads of people tried to invent the helicopter, including Leonardo da Vinci. But, as with planes, there were no powerful engines that could make them fly. In 1877, for example, French inventor Emmanuel Dieuaid tried to solve the problem by putting a steam boiler on the ground to feed a steam engine on a helicopter. But the craft couldn't fly higher than the steam pipe. So I guess it was all a pipe dream.

3 In the 1880s US inventor Thomas Edison (1847–1931) tried to solve the problem with a helicopter engine powered by explosive gun cotton. But then his lab blew up. Edison was a bright spark but he didn't need that sort of spark.

4 In the 1900s inventors began to get off the ground in their helicopters – but not more than a few metres.

5 The first really useful helicopters were inspired by Spanish inventor Juan de la Cieva, who invented the idea of a spinning rotor on top of a flying craft. By the end of the 1930s German inventor Heinrich Focke and Igor Sikorsky (yes, the guy who brought us *Le Grand*) had built their own helicopters.

Bet you never knew!
Helicopter pilots have silly slang terms for their machines. It's worth learning them so you can impress your friends by pretending to be a helicopter pilot...

BUBBLE-TOP
WHIRLYBIRD
CHOPPER
FLYING BANANA

But if you really want to be a helicopter pilot, you need to know how they work – or even how to build one yourself...

Fearsome flight fact file

NAME: How a helicopter works

THE BASIC FACTS: **1** The spinning blades or "rotors" of a helicopter work like whirling plane wings.

WHIRRR!

TAIL ROTOR

DELICIOUS!

MAIN ROTOR BLADE

PILOT EATING A BANANA IN HIS FLYING BANANA

AEROFOIL-SHAPED BLADE

2 They're aerofoil-shaped for lift and the steeper the angle of the rotors the more lift you get. By altering the angle, the pilot can make the craft rise or fall.

3 By changing the tilt of the rotors, the pilot can make the craft fly backwards, forwards or sideways.

THE FEARSOME DETAILS: **1** If a helicopter had just one set of rotors, it would spin in the same direction as the blades and everyone would get sick.

2 That's why most helicopters have a second set. They push the tail round in the opposite direction to the spin of the main rotors. Oh well, it saves on sick bags.

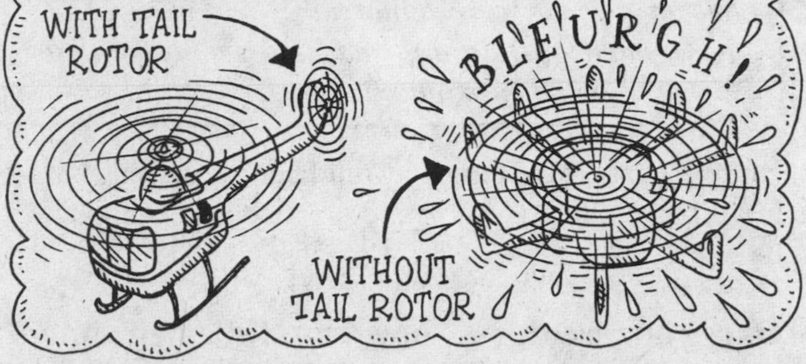

WITH TAIL ROTOR

BLEURGH!

WITHOUT TAIL ROTOR

Watch the birdie!

4 Hummingbirds and helicopters

WE HUMMINGBIRDS CAN HOVER...

UNLIKE ROTORS, OUR WINGS BEAT BACKWARDS AND FORWARDS IN A FIGURE OF EIGHT... UP TO 70 TIMES A SECOND!

OUR LONG BEAK IS HANDY FOR DRINKING NECTAR FROM FLOWERS.

I NEED A STRAW!

Hmm – I expect the burgers would be chargrilled and, all in all, I guess it's safer to build a helicopter than to try to be one…

Dare you discover … how to build a helicopter?

A QUICK NOTE TO OVER-EXCITED YOUNGER READERS

NO, it's not a real helicopter and you shouldn't try flying in it. You'll have to carry on pestering your parents if you want a real chopper for your birthday.

What you need:
Piece of paper 21 cm by 9 cm.
Ruler
Scissors (and that ever-helpful adult helper)
Paperclip
Pencil

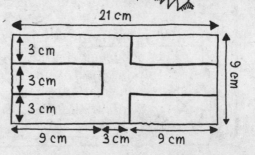

HERE WE GO AGAIN

What you do:
1 Draw the solid lines on the paper as shown.

21 cm

3 cm

3 cm

3 cm

9 cm

9 cm   3 cm   9 cm

2 Cut the paper along the solid lines.

3 Fold the paper along the dotted lines as shown. These folded bits are your rotors.

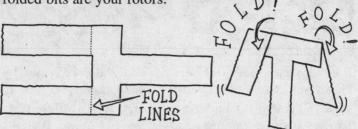

4 Now open up your rotors and slide the paperclip over the bottom end of your helicopter.

5 Ready for your first flight? Simply drop it from a height!

You should find:
The rotors spin – just like the blades of a real helicopter.

An important announcement...
Talking about building flying machines, I've just heard that our scientist buddies have built another plane. Once again they need someone to put it through its paces. So where's MI Gutzache? Oh, silly me – I forgot, he was last seen getting blown up.

As luck would have it, Gutzache and Watson escaped by parachute and were only a bit singed. And now, as I'm sure you'd love to know how to fly, we've offered MI Gutzache a vast amount of cash to teach Wanda Wye his flying skills…

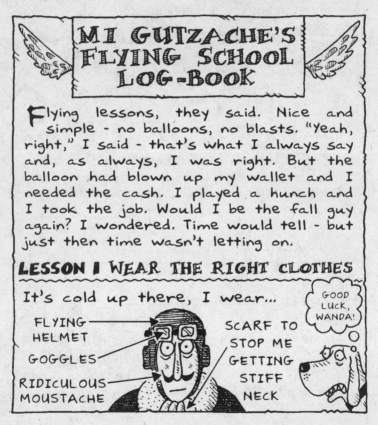

MI GUTZACHE'S FLYING SCHOOL LOG-BOOK

Flying lessons, they said. Nice and simple - no balloons, no blasts. "Yeah, right," I said - that's what I always say and, as always, I was right. But the balloon had blown up my wallet and I needed the cash. I played a hunch and I took the job. Would I be the fall guy again? I wondered. Time would tell - but just then time wasn't letting on.

LESSON I WEAR THE RIGHT CLOTHES

It's cold up there, I wear…

FLYING HELMET

GOGGLES

RIDICULOUS MOUSTACHE

SCARF TO STOP ME GETTING STIFF NECK

GOOD LUCK, WANDA!

WATERPROOF FLYING SUIT

THERMAL UNDERWEAR (UNDER JUMPERS)

TWO WOOLLY JUMPERS (UNDER SUIT)

SEVERAL PAIRS OF WOOLLY SOCKS

Things to take...

HOT-WATER BOTTLE

THERMOS AND SANDWICHES

VOMSAK SICK BAG

LUCKY CHARM

PARACHUTE - I AIN'T GOING UP WITHOUT ONE!

LESSON 2 KNOW YOUR PLANE

You've got to control the plane, or else you crash. But to do that you need to know your way around the machine...

8 PROPELLER

7 ENGINE

OK, HERE'S WHAT YOU NEED TO KNOW

1 TAIL

4 RUDDER

2 TAIL PLANE

9 FLAPS

6 AILERON

3 ELEVATOR (ONE ON EACH TAIL PLANE)

5 WING

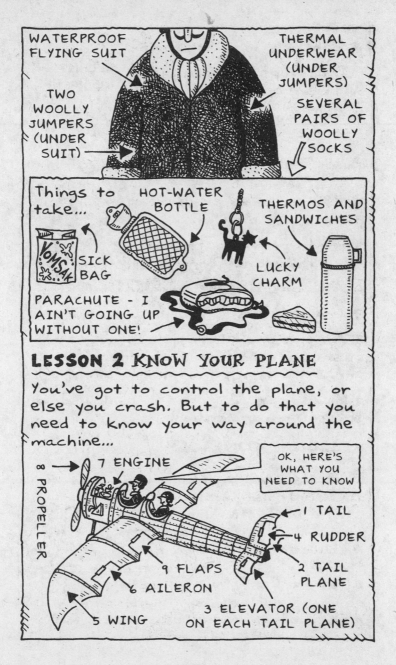

And here's what they do...

1 Tail stops the plane sliding from side to side.

2 Tail plane provides lift for the tail.

3 Elevators are used to take off, climb and dive.

4 Rudder steers the plane right or left.

5 Wings provide lift and keep the plane flying level.

6 Ailerons tilt the wings.

7 Engine powers the propeller.

8 As the propeller speeds up, it pushes air past it to produce thrust and pull the plane forwards.

9 Flaps increase drag and slow down the plane for landing.

LESSON 3 CONTROLS

It feels good to get your hands on the controls, but don't do nothing stupid with them in the air or we'll be kitty meat.

● The control column moves the ailerons and elevators.

● The brakes slow the plane down on the ground.

● The pedals move the rudder.

KITTY SNAX

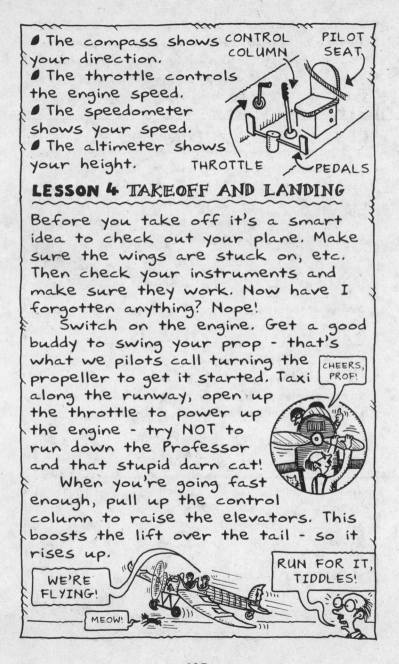

● The compass shows your direction.
● The throttle controls the engine speed.
● The speedometer shows your speed.
● The altimeter shows your height.

CONTROL COLUMN

PILOT SEAT

THROTTLE

PEDALS

LESSON 4 TAKEOFF AND LANDING

Before you take off it's a smart idea to check out your plane. Make sure the wings are stuck on, etc. Then check your instruments and make sure they work. Now have I forgotten anything? Nope!

Switch on the engine. Get a good buddy to swing your prop - that's what we pilots call turning the propeller to get it started. Taxi along the runway, open up the throttle to power up the engine - try NOT to run down the Professor and that stupid darn cat!

CHEERS, PROF!

When you're going fast enough, pull up the control column to raise the elevators. This boosts the lift over the tail - so it rises up.

WE'RE FLYING!

RUN FOR IT, TIDDLES!

MEOW!

105

To land, slow the engine and push the control column forward to lower the elevators and reduce lift. Don't forget to brake your wheels after you land!

LESSON 5 STEERING THE PLANE

You can steer the plane using the rudder pedals: left for left and right - well, you get the picture. But if you do just this, the plane skids about in the sky...

OOER!

So it makes sense to bank the plane. "Bank"... I love that word - it reminds me of wads of cash. Up here it means tilting the wings and steering the rudder at the same time. So to bank right, it's control column right and right rudder pedal down...

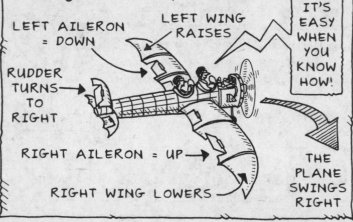

LEFT AILERON = DOWN

LEFT WING RAISES

IT'S EASY WHEN YOU KNOW HOW!

RUDDER TURNS TO RIGHT

RIGHT AILERON = UP →

RIGHT WING LOWERS

THE PLANE SWINGS RIGHT

So you'd like to learn to fly, too? Well, don't let me stop you!

Dare you discover … how to bank a plane?

What you need:

Yourself

That's it. (No, you don't need a plane – I bet you're not old enough to fly one anyway, are you?)

What you do:

1 Place your arms out straight like wings. Make sure your hands are facing down and your wings are pointing slightly upwards and well away from your granny's glass goblet collection or your dad's chin.

2 Your hands are your ailerons. Practise using them…

a) Tilt your right hand so your little finger is higher than your thumb. **b)** Tilt your left hand so your thumb is higher than your little finger. **3** Now you've raised your right aileron, your right wing (arm) should lower. And because you've lowered your left aileron, your left wing (arm) should raise. This means you can bank to the right. **4** Now try banking left.

NEEEEEEEEEEE EEEEOOOOWW WWWWWW!

You should find:

You get the hang of the controls quite quickly. Now try running around as you practise banking complete with sound effects. Just don't try it at family mealtimes … or in posh china shops.

Oh, so now you want your very own plane to practise flying in? Well, here's one that's safer than a Flying Flea and less grisly than a Gee Bee…

Dare you discover … how to build a world-beating plane?

This plane was inspired by Ralph Barnaby's winning entry in the 1967 Great International Paper Airplane competition.

What you need:
An A4 piece of paper

☠ HORRIBLE HEALTH WARNING

Do NOT use family photos or your little brother's homework for this job. Soggy toilet paper is also STRICTLY banned.

A table (it helps to do the folding on a hard surface).
Scissors (ask your local friendly adult to do the cutting).

What you do:

1 Fold the paper lengthways. Make sure the fold is nice and sharp.

2 Draw this shape and cut it out.

3 Now draw this line using a ruler. Use the ruler to make sure the line joins up with the bottom left corner.

4 Fold along the dotted line as shown.

5 Fold the front edge of the plane up as shown and then fold it twice more, as if you were rolling up a carpet.

6 Fold up the ends of the wings as shown.

7 Throw the plane *gently*. But don't absent-mindedly throw it at your brother or sister, overhead power line, priceless family heirlooms or the dog.

8 Now cut an aileron on each wing, like so...

9 And an elevator on each half of the tail, like so...

10 Try throwing your plane with the controls set in different ways.

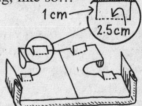

You should find:

The ailerons and elevators work just like the plane Gutzache was flying on page 106. Well, a bit better actually.

Mind you, it doesn't matter how well your plane flies – it's not going anywhere without someone to fly it. Someone brave and fearless who doesn't mind risking their neck. In the early days of flight, pilots had to be barmy or brave to fly at all ... but are you brave enough to read about them?

POTTY PIONEER PILOTS

OK, so it was a bad idea to throw a pioneer pilots' party. The wacko wing-nuts are showing off and swinging from the light fittings and doing handstands on the windowsills. But then I guess if you risk your life to fly it helps if you're a little loopy…

> **Bet you never knew!**
> In 1922, star US pilot Jimmy Doolittle did handstands on a windowsill at a party in Chile. He fell, breaking both his ankles – but that didn't stop him putting on an awesome air display a few days later.

Anyway, we've got to make our excuses and dash off for France in 1909, where a pair of fearless fliers are about to race for glory … or death.

Time for a Channel chase (again!)

Inspired by the sight of Wilbur Wright flying with ease, the European flying freaks began to build better planes and set their sights on a new goal. Just as in the early days of ballooning, the race was on to fly the English Channel and win £10,000 from a British newspaper. Here are the front runners – who do you fancy to win?

DATE	Name: LOUIS BLÉRIOT	Name: HERBERT LATHAM
1906	I'm a rich car headlamp maker.	I'm a rich thrill-seeker.
1908	I've spent all my money building planes that crash.	I've got a deadly lung disease. I don't mind if I die!
1909	If I don't win the prize, I'll be ruined!	I'm going to fly the Channel - or die!
19 JULY	Wait! I'm not ready yet!	Grr - I tried to fly but I crashed into the sea!
23 JULY	I've burnt my foot! I can't sleep!	Wake me up at 3.30 am to fly!
24 JULY 3.30 am	Time to go!	ZZZZZZZ.
4.50 am	OH NO, I'm lost and my engine's overheating! Phew! It's raining. That'll cool it down.	Grr - why didn't you wake me up? Now it's too late to catch Blériot!

HURRAH — I've won! I've arrived in England!

Good morning!

GRRRR - I'VE LOST!

Bet you never knew!
1 Blériot was cheered by a crowd as he landed. And then he was questioned by a miserable customs official, who thought he was a smuggler.
2 The future held very different fortunes for our two fearless fliers. Blériot made another fortune as a plane maker – everyone wanted to buy his channel-flying plane, the Blériot XI. Latham went big-game hunting and got gored to death by a charging buffalo.

THIS IS ONE CHARGE I CAN'T AFFORD!

The race across the Channel wasn't the only risky race around. In 1911 a US newspaper boss offered $50,000 to the first pilot to fly across the USA in 30 days. Pilot Calbraith Rodgers tried to win the prize, but on the way he suffered…

- 16 crashes.
- Including five really BIG crashes.
- And used enough spare parts to build *four* planes.

His worst crash was just 19 km from the sea. He wrecked his plane, spent weeks in hospital with a broken leg and didn't win the prize. The next year he went back to the area and crashed after smacking into a seagull. Rodgers died and the seagull probably hopped the twig too.

But even without the perils of racing, pilots were crashing and dying in fearsome numbers. In just one year, 1910, 37 pilots were killed in crashes. And that was a fair proportion of all the people who could fly at the time!

Four ways to nearly kill yourself if you're an early flier

1 The death dive

The Wrights' *Flyer* had an awkward problem, shared with most planes. It stalled. If you tried to fly upwards too steeply, the air moving over the wing flowed less smoothly and slowed down. The wings lost lift and the plane spiralled down and crashed.

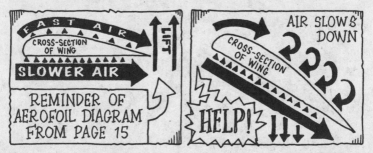

In 1912, top test pilot Harry Hawker had the idea of *steepening* the dive as the plane fell. This slowed the plane's speed and allowed the pilot to pull out of the dive. But the only way Hawker could test his hunch was to try it. He was right. Had he been wrong, it would have been less of a hunch and more of a CRUNCH!

2 Stunt flying

Stunt flying attracts the real winged wackos – folk like Lincoln Beachey, nicknamed "the Flying Fool". His tricks included:

• Flying *under* bridges.
• Flying along a street over the heads of passers-by.
• When a group of people climbed a tree to see one of his shows for free, Lincoln buzzed the tree so they fell out.

All of this was deeply dangerous and luckless Lincoln lost his life in 1915 in front of 50,000 people.

Bet you never knew!
In 1910 the Wright brothers set up a flying team to show off their planes, but all but one of the team were killed. The survivor's name was Frank Coffyn.

3 Wing walking

But there's one sport that makes stunt flying sound as sensible as a pair of boring old lace-up shoes. It was started by potty US pilot Ormer Locklear and to do it you had to walk on the wings of your plane – *while it was in the air*! Or hang from the wheels by your teeth. Or leap to another plane.

Now that's plane crazy, but after the First World War, scores of out-of-work pilots tried it for a living – or dying. And Ormer ended up crashing into a pool of sludgy oil – so he came to a sticky end.

Sorry, readers, you'll have to read this next bit standing on your head. Or you could try flying your plane upside down!

4 Flying upside down

This was pioneered by Russian pilot Petr Nesterov, the first man to loop the loop. The loopy army pilot was rewarded with ten days in prison for risking government property. By the 1930s, upside-down flying was a curious craze and Italian pilot Tito Falconi even flew 420 km from St Louis to Chicago the wrong way up.

Clearly, life for the first pilots was a bit of a gamble and they weren't exactly good risks for life insurance. But at least it was peaceful… In time of war, a pilot's life became even more dangerous…

The deadly demands of war

What is it with humans? No sooner do they invent something than they want to use it to kill each other. In 1917 Orville Wright said that when he and his brother built the world's first plane…

We thought we were introducing into the world an invention that would make future wars practically impossible…

HOW WRONG THEY WERE! Just look at this…

The fearsome fight for fighting flight

1914–1918 First World War. British, French and American pilots battle with German pilots in the air. The Germans lose because they have fewer planes and pilots.
1939 War breaks out again. The German Air Force rules the skies.
1940 Britain's RAF saves the country from German invasion by shooting down more German planes than it loses.

1940–1942 The Germans bomb British cities instead.

1942–1945 The British and Americans bomb German cities.

1942–1945 American and Japanese planes take off from aircraft carriers to fight vast battles across the Pacific. The Americans win.

In the First World War the life of a fighter pilot was exciting and glorious … and short. In 1915 a British pilot in France could expect to live just 11 days and pilots were sent into battle with just five hours of flying experience. The British, French or American pilots weren't even allowed parachutes because they might try to escape from their plane rather than fight.

Here's a song by the American squadron in France that you might like sing at school dinners (adding "boy" or "girl" instead of "man").

So stand by your glasses steady
The world is a web of lies
Here's a toast for the dead already
Hurrah for the next man who dies!

Nearly one in three of the brave American pilots were killed – but hopefully your mouldy mashed potato and cabbage aren't quite so dangerous.

But the story of flight in the twentieth century wasn't all doom and destruction. In the 1920s, trail-blazing pilots opened new air routes. These pilots included famous female fliers such as...

• American Amelia Earhart (1898–1937), the first woman to fly the Atlantic in 1928. She was actually a passenger but she amused herself by trying to drop oranges on the head of the captain of a passing ship.

She missed. Four years later she made the trip on her own.

• Briton Amy Johnson (1903–1941), the first woman to fly on her own from Britain to Australia. She also flew the length of Africa and across Asia and lots of other places.

So would you want to sign up for these pioneering flights? Well, they might prove a hair-raising holiday...

HONEST BOB'S HOLIDAYS PRESENTS...

FABULOUS FLIGHTS TO FARAWAY PLACES... YOU'LL BE THE FIRST ONE TO DO IT! HEY, IT'S AN ADVENTURE AND YOU'LL REMEMBER IT FOR THE REST OF YOUR LIFE (AND THAT MAY NOT BE VERY LONG – OOPS, PRETEND I NEVER SAID THAT!)

FREE CRASH COURSE IN FLYING WITH EVERY HOLIDAY SOLD!

I NEWFOUNDLAND TO IRELAND (1919)

As flown by John Alcock (1892–1919) and Arthur Whitten Brown (1886–1948)

HOPE YOU CAN READ MAPS

HOPE YOU CAN SWIM

- First World War bomber with open cockpit. Lots of lovely fresh freezing air and a hard wooden bench to sit on (it's good for your bum!).
- Experience the first non-stop flight across the Atlantic Ocean. Relive the drama as your radio aerial falls off, so you can't call for help if things go wrong!

- Enjoy lots of exercise as you climb onto the wings to remove ice.
- Free sandwiches.
- All this, plus a thrilling crash landing in an Irish bog!

WELL, YOU SAID YOU NEEDED THE BOG!

PLOOP!

2 THE CHUBBIE MILLER AND BILL LANCASTER WORLD TOUR – Britain to Australia (1928)

It's a thrill a minute as you...

- Find a poisonous snake in your plane in Rangoon.
- Crash in Muntok. (Don't worry if you get a couple of black eyes and a smashed plane – hey, it's all part of the fun!)
- Get your very own de-luxe runway built by prisoners so you can take off from a jail at Attambre.
- Nearly crash into the Timor Sea and get eaten by sharks. You can write a farewell letter at this point (free stamp).

I'M CHUBBIE

AND I'M QUITE THIN

THE SMALL PRINT – When you get to Australia no one takes much notice of you because another flyer's already made the trip. And you're not allowed to leave your plane until you've been checked for tropical diseases.

3 THE LINDBERGH SPECIAL
– New York to Paris (1927)

Need a little peace and quiet? Well, here's the flight for you! It's only 33 hours but you do it all on your own!

- Lovely break in Paris when you get there – if you get there.
- Your plane has no radio so you don't have to talk to anyone – even if you want to call for help! (Some pilots end up chatting to themselves.)

FANCY A SANDWICH? THANKS, DON'T MIND IF I DO! WHAT'S IN THEM? FISHPASTE. LOVELY!

THE SMALL PRINT
Just make sure you don't fall asleep – or you'll crash and die. By 1927 five pilots had died trying to make this flight.

Lindbergh kept himself awake by slapping his face, bouncing in his seat and sticking his hands out of the window. And by the time he landed in Paris, he probably needed a good night's snooze. He woke up to find himself a world mega-star. He was so incredibly famous...

- The US Government sent a warship to pick him up.
- He got a gold medal from the US Congress.
- He met Orville Wright.

But Charles was so modest and polite that everyone thought he was the best thing since apple pie AND custard.

Lindbergh's famous flight had made flying fab and fashionable like nothing else could. People queued to train as pilots, and passengers queued to fly to the remote parts of the world opened up by pioneer pilots. But what really made passenger flight take off (geddit?) was a new engine that could carry people faster than ever before. Today this engine powers most of the world's passenger planes and we're about to jet off to find out more about it.

Hmm – it's rather noisy. Maybe you'd better put on a pair of these before you read on...

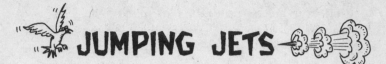

JUMPING JETS

If you've ever flown, the chances are you've flown in a jet plane. This chapter is about how the jet engine was invented and how it changed flying for ever. But first let's check out the basics about this marvellous machine...

Fearsome flight fact file

NAME: Jet engines

THE BASIC FACTS: **1** Jet engines suck in air and blast it out behind them. This has the effect of driving the engine – and the plane – forward.

AIR SUCKED IN

AIR BLASTED OUT

SUCK!

BLAST!

VRRRT! PARDON ME!

THE CAPTAIN'S SUFFERING FROM "JET-BOTTOM"

2 They're faster and more powerful than propeller engines. And that meant that designers could build bigger passenger planes and more people got a chance to fly.

ONE MAN AND HIS DOG

MORE THAN 400 PEOPLE!

THE FEARSOME DETAILS: 1 Jet engines can suck in birds and fail. In 1960, 62 people died in Boston, USA, when their plane hit a flock of starlings.

2 Today jet engines are tested by firing dead birds into them with a special cannon. If the engines stop, they fail the test.

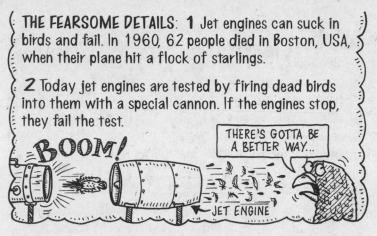

Now, I bet you're wondering who actually came up with the whizzy, wonderful jet engine. Well, as ever in horrible science, the answer is confusingly complicated. It really is a question to stupefy a scientist…

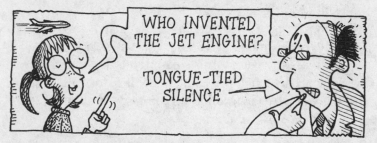

You see, crowds of inventors had the idea and some of them even designed jet engines that *nearly* worked. I bet if they all met up there'd be a fearsome punch-up over who got the glory…

The fearsome fight for jet engines

1st century AD Hero, a Greek scientist from Alexandria in Egypt, invents a device that whizzes round, powered by jets of steam. It's not a jet engine but it works in the same way.

1783 Joseph Montgolfier thinks about letting the air out of a balloon so it will whizz off with a rude sound, like a toy balloon. There wasn't enough air pressure in the balloon for this – worse luck!

1791 Inventor John Barber cooks up an engine powered by burning gas. But it's not powerful enough to be much use and anyway he wants to use it in ships.

1837 Sir George Cayley dreams of an air-powered engine – but he never builds it. Too busy as usual, no doubt.

All these inventors missed out on the jumping jet engine, so let's jet our time machine forward to the 1930s, when two incredible inventors were about to grab a bigger slice of the action...

Bet you never knew!
British inventor Frank Whittle (1907–1996) had the idea for the jet engine while studying at flying college in 1929, but his teacher didn't take his brainwave seriously. So, in 1936, Whittle set up his own company to make the new engine, but the British government didn't take him seriously either. Until the Second World War broke out and a fast jet fighter plane suddenly seemed like a good idea...

The incredible thing was that German inventor Hans von Ohain (1911–1998) was also working on the jet engine. The two inventors knew nothing of each other, so we've let them tell their stories separately.

Frank Whittle's story	Hans von Ohain's story

DATE

1939 — At last, my government has ordered one plane with my jet engine! | At last, my government has ordered two planes with my jet engine!

1941 — My plane flies perfectly. | My two planes fly perfectly.

1944 — Hurrah! My jets are fighting the enemy and they're winning. | Grr – my jets are fighting the enemy, but they're dangerous to fly.

HOORAY!!

ERK!

The secret life of the jumping jet engine

And now to find out the innermost secrets of how jet engines work – and a vital new word…

Fearsome expressions

A scientist says…

I'M KEEN ON TURBINES

Do you say…?

YUCK – I HATE THEM IN SOUP!

Answer:
NO, they're turbines not TURNIPS! A turbine is a sort of spinning fan with angled blades. Turbines produce electricity and power boats and they're vital for jet engines.

It so happens that Professor N Large and Wanda Wye have added a couple of jet engines to their plane. And that's handy because it means we'll be able to see the engines in action. Er, we'd better hurry – Gutzache is just taking off…

WHAAAAAA!

ZEOW!

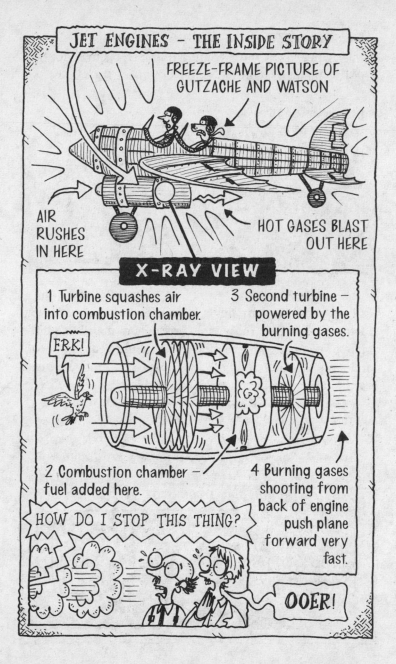

JET ENGINES — THE INSIDE STORY

FREEZE-FRAME PICTURE OF GUTZACHE AND WATSON

AIR RUSHES IN HERE

HOT GASES BLAST OUT HERE

X-RAY VIEW

1 Turbine squashes air into combustion chamber.

ERK!

3 Second turbine — powered by the burning gases.

2 Combustion chamber — fuel added here.

4 Burning gases shooting from back of engine push plane forward very fast.

HOW DO I STOP THIS THING?

OOER!

Horrible holidays

Well, if that hadn't put you off flying, let's find out how the jet plane changed the way passengers fly…

Spot the difference competition…

In the 1920s, when flights began between London and Cologne, Germany, only eight passengers could fit on the plane. The plane was so noisy no one could hear you speak, and it shook so alarmingly that the passengers were given cans to throw up in. Oh yes, and the plane had no toilet…

Bet you never knew!
I bet you're wondering how the old-style pilots managed in the days before there were toilets on planes. Well, they held on and if they couldn't… In 1931 US pilot Bobbie Trout used an old coffee can.

By the 1950s, passengers could relax on large jet planes (with toilets) and the jet engine provided a smoother flight. But flying could still be a fearsome experience. You had to be *really brave* to fly in some early jets…

Could you be a scientist?

In 1954, Britain's new Comet jets had an annoying habit of falling to bits in the air and crashing.

1 How did scientists find the cause of the crashes?

a) They built a new plane and flew in it.

b) They put the plane in a giant pool and pumped it full of water.

c) They let a bad-tempered elephant wreck the plane and inspected the damage very carefully.

2 What proved to be the problem?

a) The wings were only glued on.

b) The plane was rusty.

c) The square windows had cracked at the corners.

Answers:

1 b) The sides of the plane were too thin. Jet planes fly fastest at heights where the air is thin and causes less drag. But that means air has to be pumped into the cabin so the passengers won't gasp and black out for lack of air to breathe.

… BUT DON'T PUMP TOO MUCH!

THE PASSENGERS ARE COMPLAINING THAT THERE'S TOO MUCH ROOM, CAPTAIN

The changes in air pressure weakened the plane and the scientists found this out by increasing the pressure of the water on the plane.

2 c) And the weakest point was the corner of the windows.

Bet you never knew!
Modern jets are far stronger. For example, the sides of a jumbo jet are 19 cm thick and the windows are toughened glass as thick as your fist.

Teacher's tea-break teaser
Tap lightly on the staffroom door. When your teacher appears, smile sweetly and ask them...

Your teacher will crossly inform you that a Boeing 747 *is* a jumbo jet. This is true – jumbo jet is a nickname for the plane – but you can say...

By the 1970s flying was an everyday event – in 1977 nearly two-thirds of Americans had flown … in the previous year! And air travel has continued to grow. Today, jets fly millions of passengers all over the world. And there's even a choice of jet engines…

• Ordinary plain old turbo-jet engines, like the ones on Gutzache's plane.

• Turbo-fan engines, used in large jets. A fan draws air into the engine and wafts some air round the combustion chamber to keep it cool.

• Turbo-prop or prop-fan engines, which combine turbines with propellers.

Bet you never knew!

Some jet engines can be turned downwards to make a plane hover in mid-air! They're used on the Harrier jump-jet fighter. When the engines were tested in the 1950s, engineers built a thingie known as the "flying bedstead" that hovered in mid-air. In 1957 it killed a test pilot. Fancy a snooze on a flying bedstead?

HOVER!

IT SOUNDS MORE LIKE A NIGHTMARE!

And by the 1970s there was another type of plane to fly in. A plane that travelled faster than your VOICE and made the jumbo jet look like a slug with a wooden leg. Yes, this next bit is sure to take the words out of your mouth…

Fearsome flight fact file

NAME: Supersonic jets

THE BASIC FACTS: 1 Imagine your teacher telling you to go home early. The sound of her voice actually reaches your ears at 1,220 km per hour. And that's only slightly slower than the class leaving the classroom.

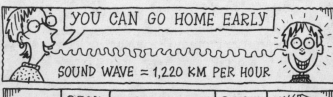

YOU CAN GO HOME EARLY

SOUND WAVE ≈ 1,220 KM PER HOUR

DESK — WHOOSH! — DOOR

CLASS LEAVING = 1,221 KM PER HOUR

2 Jets that fly faster than sound travel faster than the air can get out of the way. The air builds up in front of the plane like a wall – it's called the sound barrier. Once through this wall, the flight is smoother.

STAND BY FOR A BIG BANG...

YOU MEAN, THE SONIC BOOM AS WE BREAK THE SOUND BARRIER?

NO, THE LOUD BOOM WHEN WE HIT THAT MOUNTAIN

3 Supersonic planes are streamlined to reduce drag. They have swept-back, "delta-shaped" wings so the wing hits the sound barrier at an angle rather than straight on. This makes the ride less bumpy.

THE FEARSOME DETAILS: In 1946 British pilot Geoffrey de Havilland Jr died trying to break the sound barrier. Sadly it broke his plane to bits. The first pilot to do the feat was US pilot Chuck Yeager in 1947.

G de Havilland

Chuck Yeager

Watch the birdie!
5 Birds that fly fast

WE HAWKS HAVE WINGS SHAPED LIKE A JET.

ITS SHAPE GIVES ME LIFT WITHOUT TOO MUCH DRAG...

LIKE SOME JETS, I CAN FOLD MY WINGS BACK FOR A MORE STREAMLINED SHAPE.

SWEPT-BACK WING

POINTED SHAPE

THEN I DIVE AT 180 KM PER HOUR. OK, SO IT'S NOT AS FAST AS A JET...

ERK! BUT IT'S FAST ENOUGH TO CATCH ME!

But you could interest your parents in a vintage classic plane from the 1970s. Concorde was a supersonic passenger jet developed in Britain and France, and it so happens that Honest Bob's got one for sale...

HONEST BOB'S PLANE PRODUCTS PRESENTS...

CONCORDE They don't make Concordes like they used to. Well, they don't make them at all! But just look what you get for your £50,999,999 (bring the money in a suitcase and don't ask awkward questions).
Top speed = 2,333 km per hour.
Gold-plated windows cut down on harmful rays from the sun.

PARACHUTE TO SLOW IT DOWN FOR LANDING

NOSE DROOPS ON TAKEOFF AND LANDING SO THE PILOTS CAN SEE WHERE THEY'RE GOING

MY NOSE ISN'T DROOPY!

NO TAIL PLANE

ELEVONS = COMBINED AILERONS AND ELEVATORS

136

The vital facts that somehow slipped Bob's mind

1 Concorde was so noisy that it was banned from flying over many countries.

2 In a bid to make the plane quieter, it flew at 800 km per hour over land. But then it used fuel eight times more quickly than a normal jet plane.

A fantastic future in the air?

So what do the next 50 years hold for the future of flight? Er, well, I'd love to give you the lowdown on tomorrow's high-flyers, but sadly I can't. My crystal ball is cracked and my tea leaves have dribbled down the sink... And anyway, the fearsome fight for flight is full of obscure inventors who suddenly pop up with machines that no one believed possible.

But we can take a look at some cutting-edge, state-of-the-art aircraft that might just become more common in years to come. They're built from new materials called composites (com-po-sits). These substances are made up of two different materials such as carbon and kevlar, and they're very light and strong. So they're a plane-designer's dream...

Honest Bob is selling the planes, but he's just bumped his head and now he's a changed man... He's actually become honest!

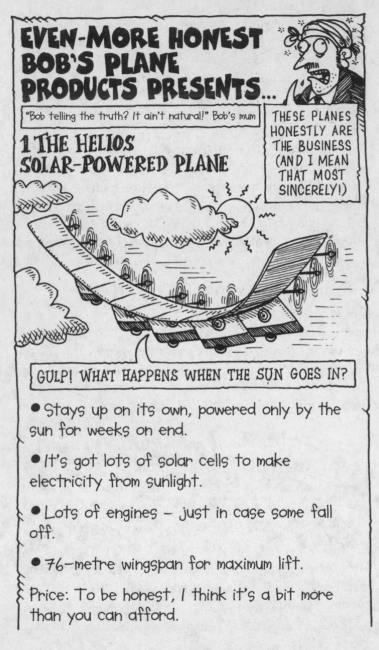

EVEN-MORE HONEST BOB'S PLANE PRODUCTS PRESENTS...

"Bob telling the truth? It ain't natural!" Bob's mum

THESE PLANES HONESTLY ARE THE BUSINESS (AND I MEAN THAT MOST SINCERELY!)

1 THE HELIOS SOLAR-POWERED PLANE

GULP! WHAT HAPPENS WHEN THE SUN GOES IN?

- Stays up on its own, powered only by the sun for weeks on end.

- It's got lots of solar cells to make electricity from sunlight.

- Lots of engines – just in case some fall off.

- 76–metre wingspan for maximum lift.

Price: To be honest, I think it's a bit more than you can afford.

2 THE GLOBAL HAWK

If you're into radio planes, this is the machine for you!

TEATIME!

HANG ON, MUM. I'M FLYING OVER RUSSIA

- You can fly it from your computer on the other side of the world.
- Super-sensitive spy cameras can spot your teacher's underpants on the washing line from 74 km away. It's your very own spy in the sky!
- As used by the US military.
- It's even got a self-destruct programme.

Price: I'll do you the cheapest price I can – but it's still a bit steep!

3 THE GOSSAMER ALBATROSS PEDAL-POWERED PLANE

CHOMP! MUNCH! HMM, NICE CHOC!

HE'S FILLING HIS ENGINE WITH FUEL

- Lovely pedal-powered plane made of plastic and piano wire.
- 30-metre wing span for maximum lift.
- Three-metre propeller powered by your pedals.
- Guaranteed not to fly more than a few metres in the air, so you won't get hurt if it crashes.

Price: Unlike the plane ... it's too high!

Yes, at last humans had achieved the ultimate dream of muscle-powered flight. But hold on … a human flying from Crete? Isn't that how the fearsome fight for flight began?

THANKS FOR REMINDING ME!

EPILOGUE: FATEFUL FLIGHT

As Jacques Charles lifted off in his hydrogen balloon in 1785, wise old American scientist Benjamin Franklin (1706–1790) was among the crowd. A man next to him asked, "What's the use of it?"
Franklin replied…

No, silly! Franklin didn't mean that flying would only be good for eating, dribbling, crying and other unmentionable baby behaviour. He meant that, like a baby, flight was the start of something new and exciting. Something that would grow and grow. And boy was he right!

Flying has proved to be the biggest success story in the history of the world. It's changed the lives of countless millions of people in an incredibly short time…

• The first engine-powered plane flight happened in 1903. Just 44 years later, humans were flying faster than sound. It all happened inside a human lifetime.

• Just five people saw the *Flyer's* first flight. There was no airfield except a pair of rails that cost $5.

• Today there are airports all over the planet and the biggest ones, such as King Khalid Airport in Saudi Arabia, are larger than small countries. (It's four times bigger than the entire island of Bermuda.)

• The *Flyer* flew no higher than a budgie and no faster than a racing bicycle.

• Today's fastest planes can zoom 16 km in the air at the speed of a rifle bullet. In 2004 US scientists tested a robot plane than could fly at *seven times* the speed of sound.

• In 1903 most letters were carried on carts pulled by wheezy old horses. Today a letter can sent anywhere on Earth and arrive in days by air. And where letters go, so can people.

Planes ... the good news
1 Flying has helped millions of people visit new parts of the world and make new friends in other countries.
2 Flying has brought food and medicines to hungry and sick people in disaster areas.
3 Scientists have gained the chance to study pollution and rocks and mountains and wild animals from the air. In terms of what flying can do, the sky really is the limit and yet ... and yet.

Planes ... the fearsome news

1 As more and more people fly, airports are getting overcrowded.

2 There's more noise and more pollution and more danger of planes bashing into each other as they wait to land.

3 Planes have killed thousands of people by bombing.

People paid a fearsome price to fly. Experts reckon that even before the *Flyer's* first flight, 200 men were killed trying to fly with wacko wings, barmy balloons and grisly gliders. But then flying is a bit like science. You can't say it's either good or bad – it's what you do with it that counts. Happy Horrible Science, everyone!

WINNER of the Junior Aventis
Science Book Prize 2004